WE RECOMMEND PUTTING A BLANK SHEET OF PAPER BEHIND YOUR ARTWORK WHEN USING MARKERS TO PREVENT BLEED THROUGH.

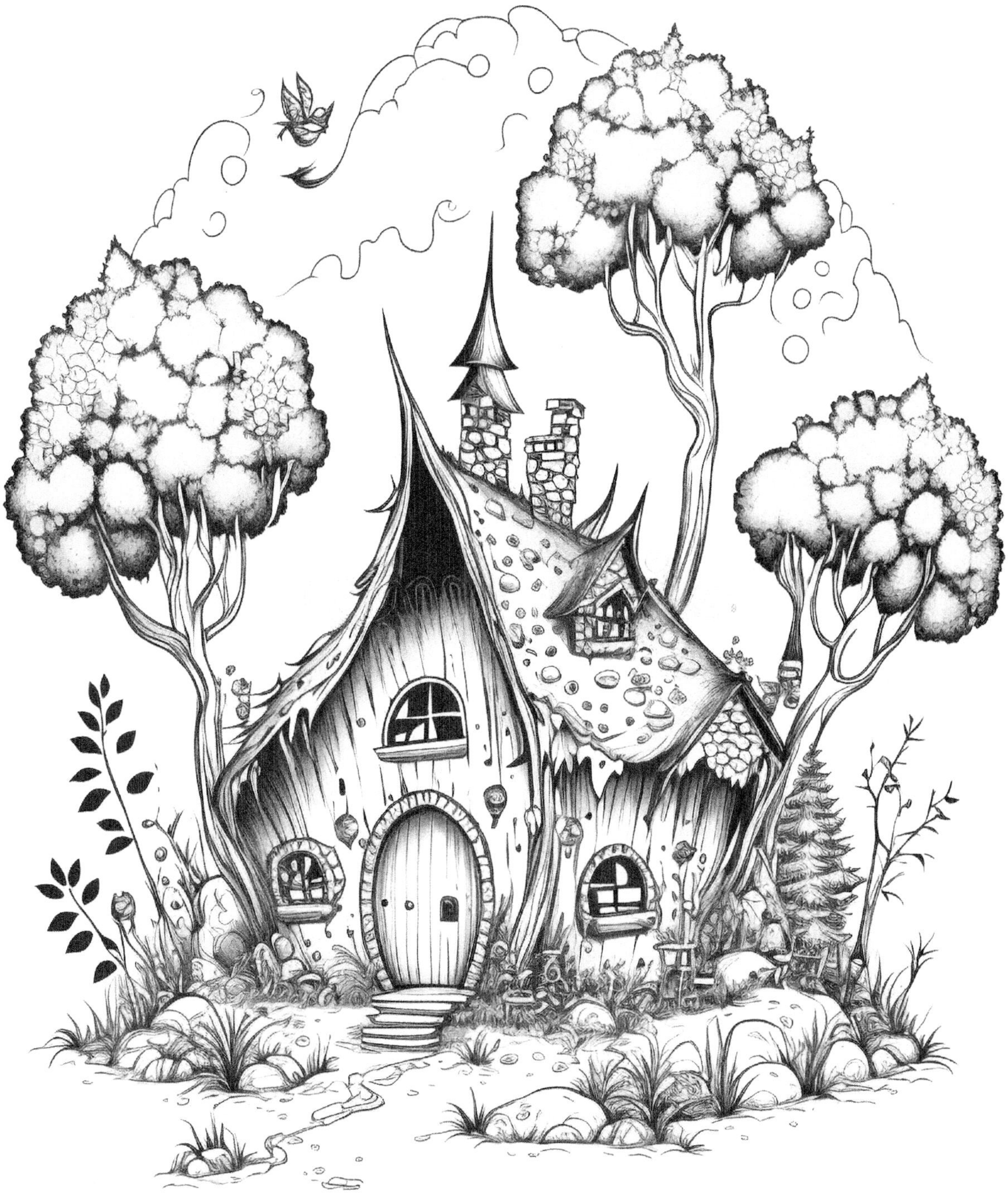

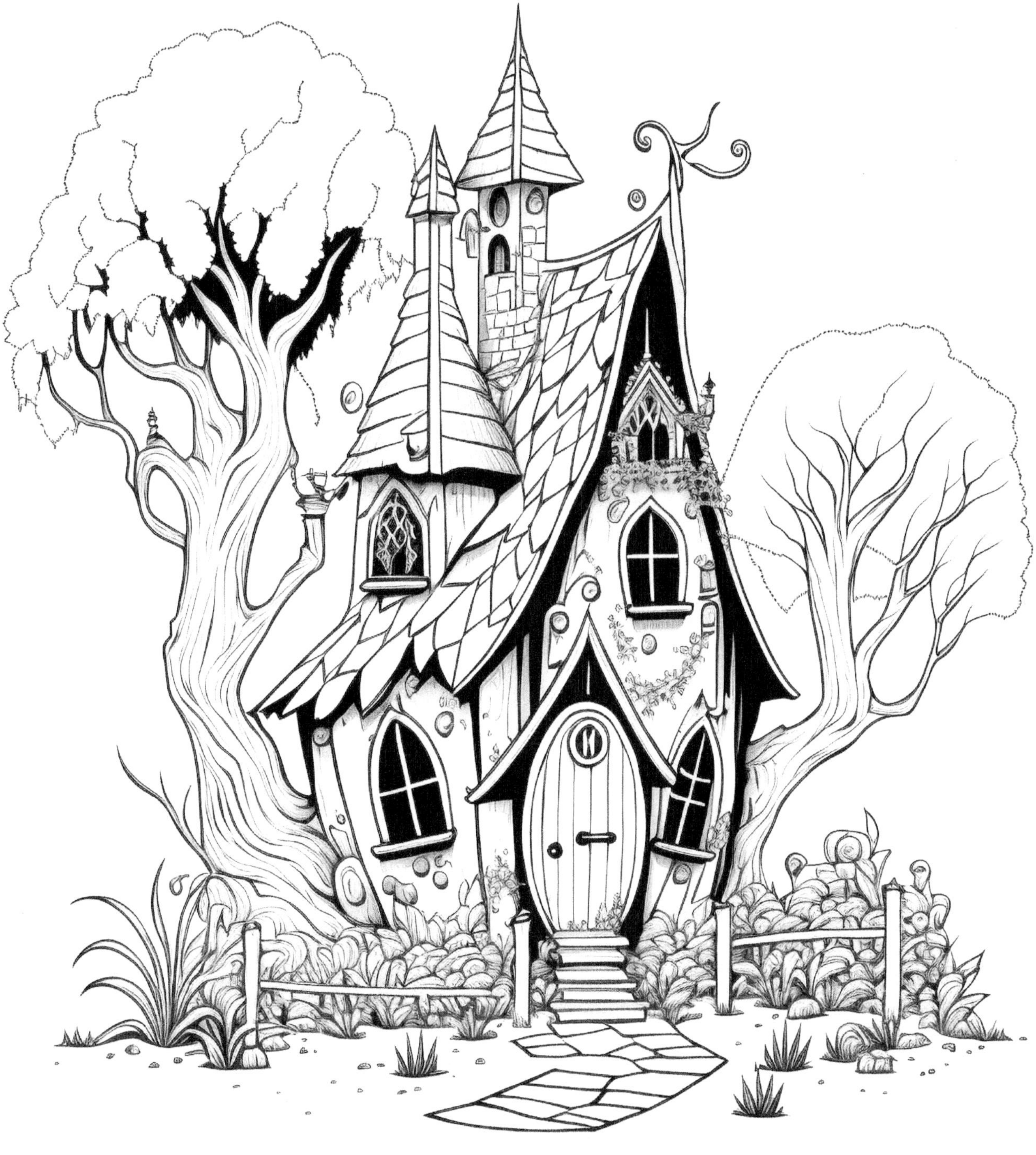

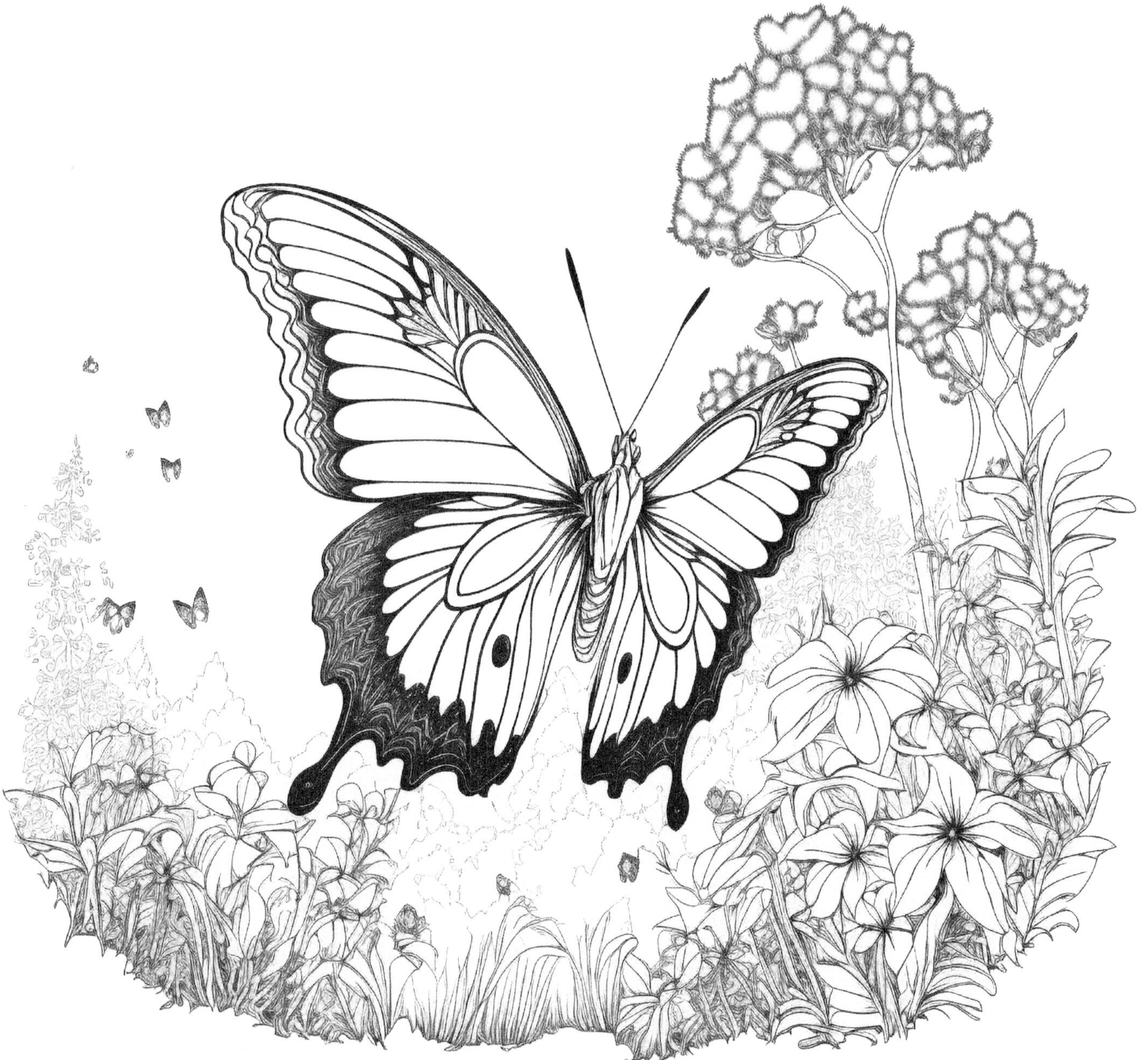

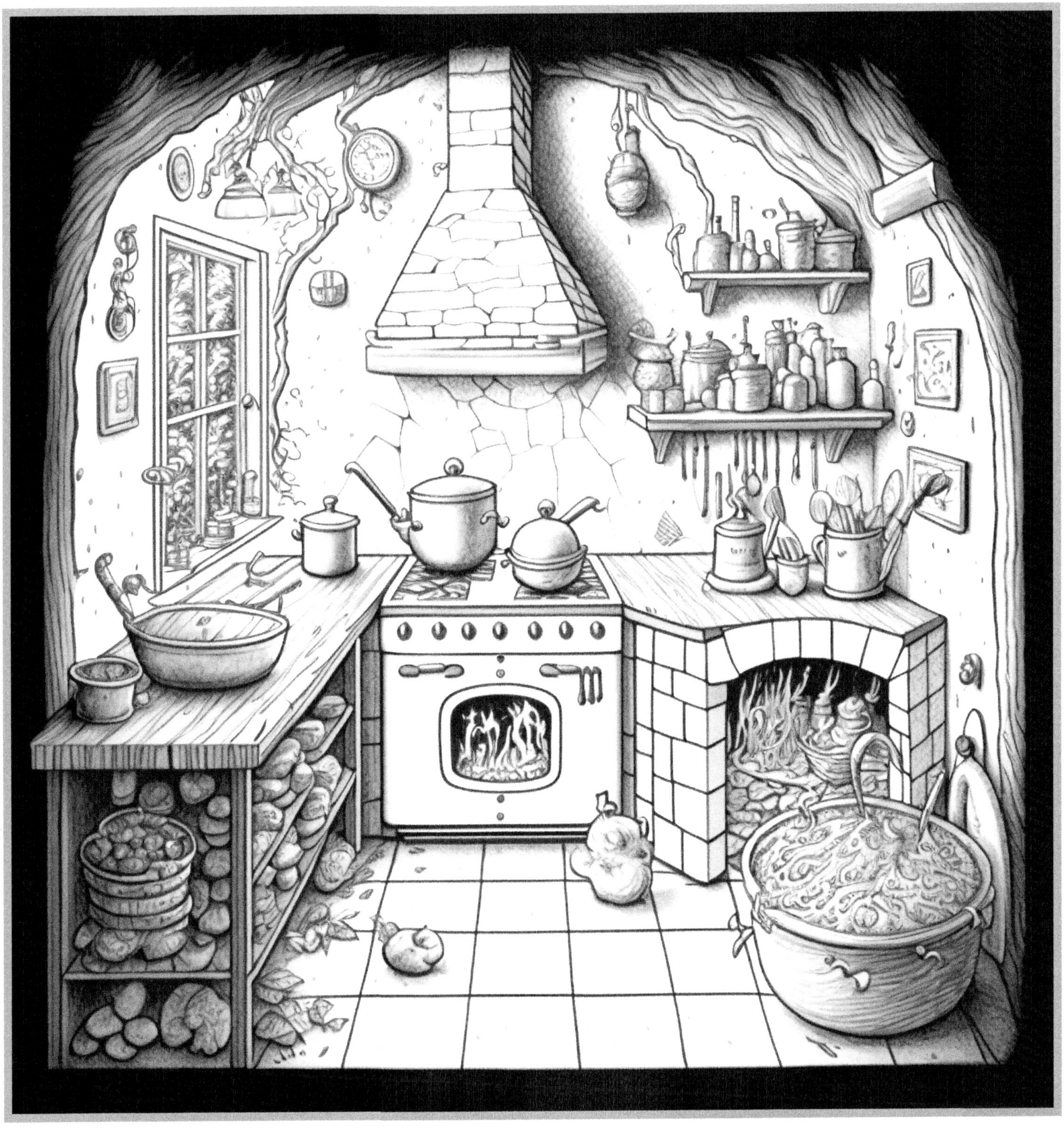

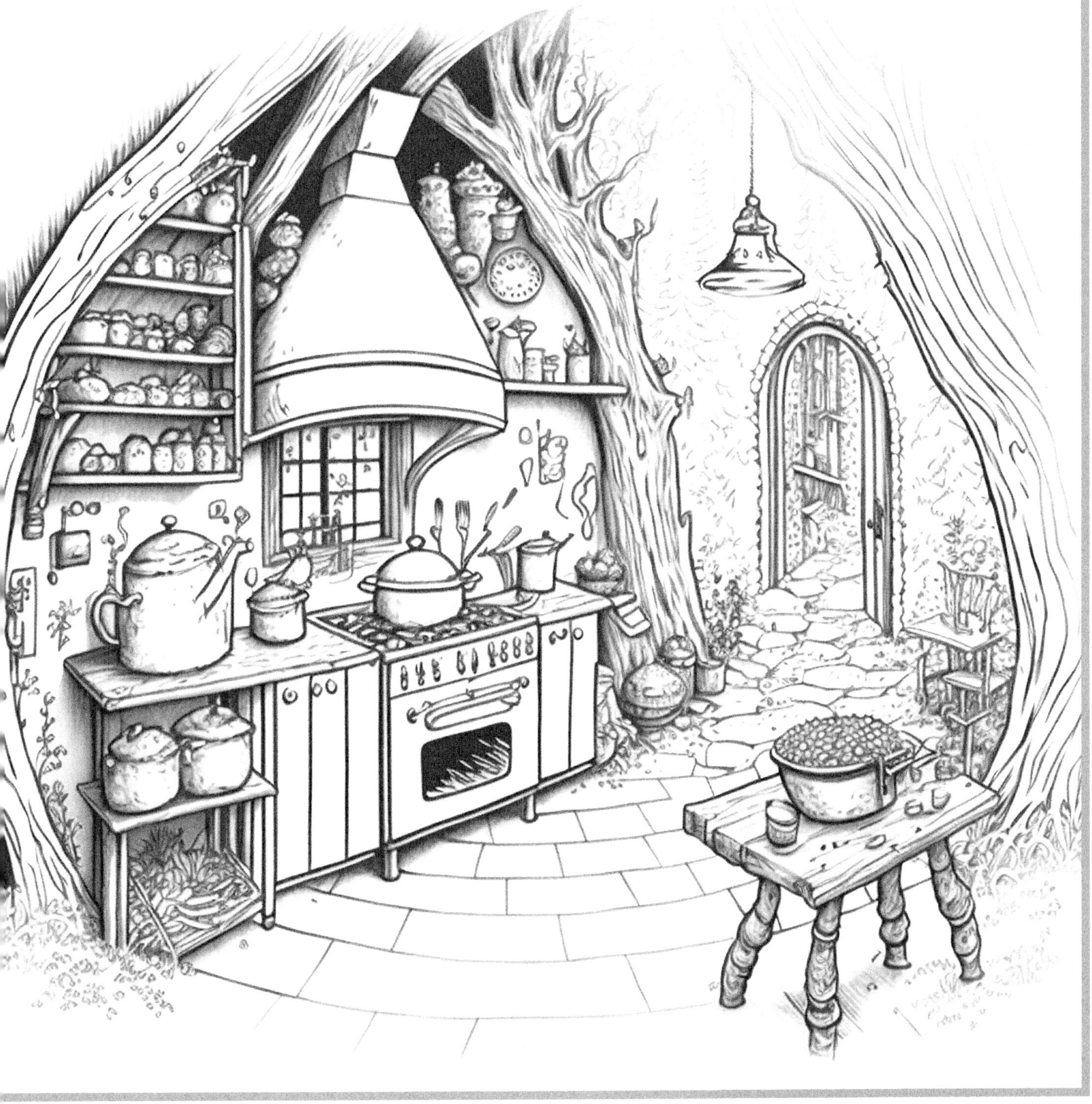

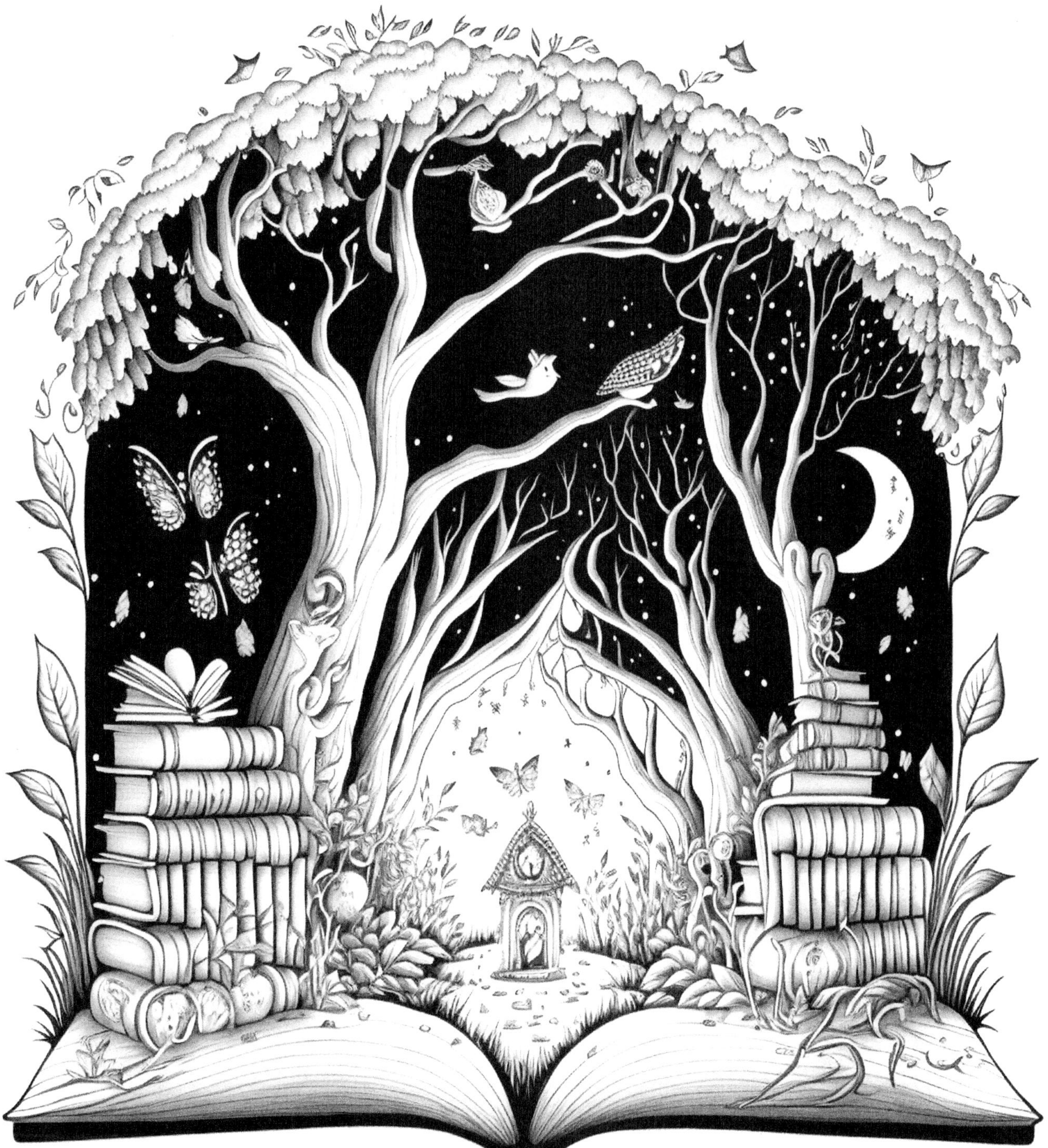

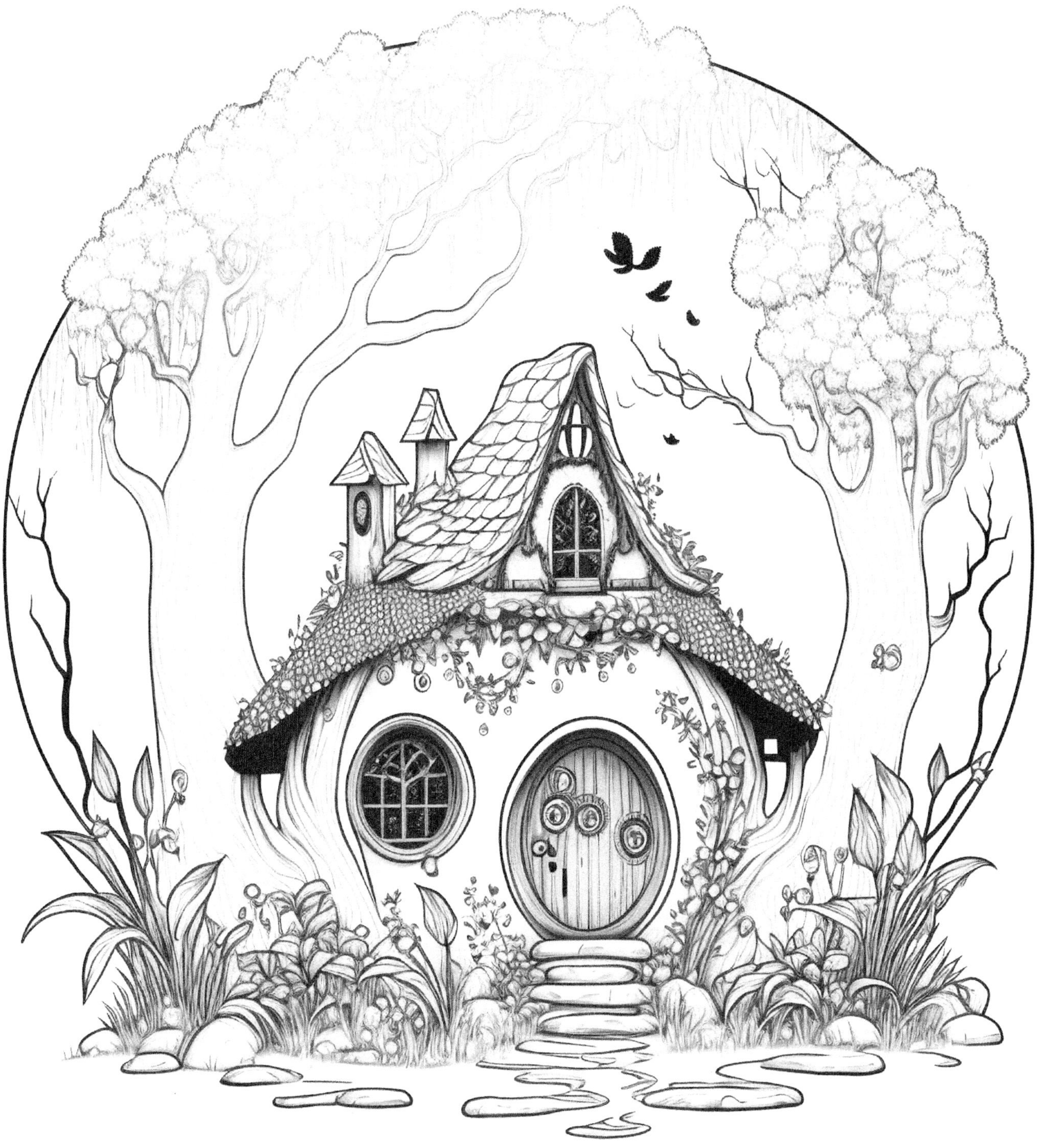

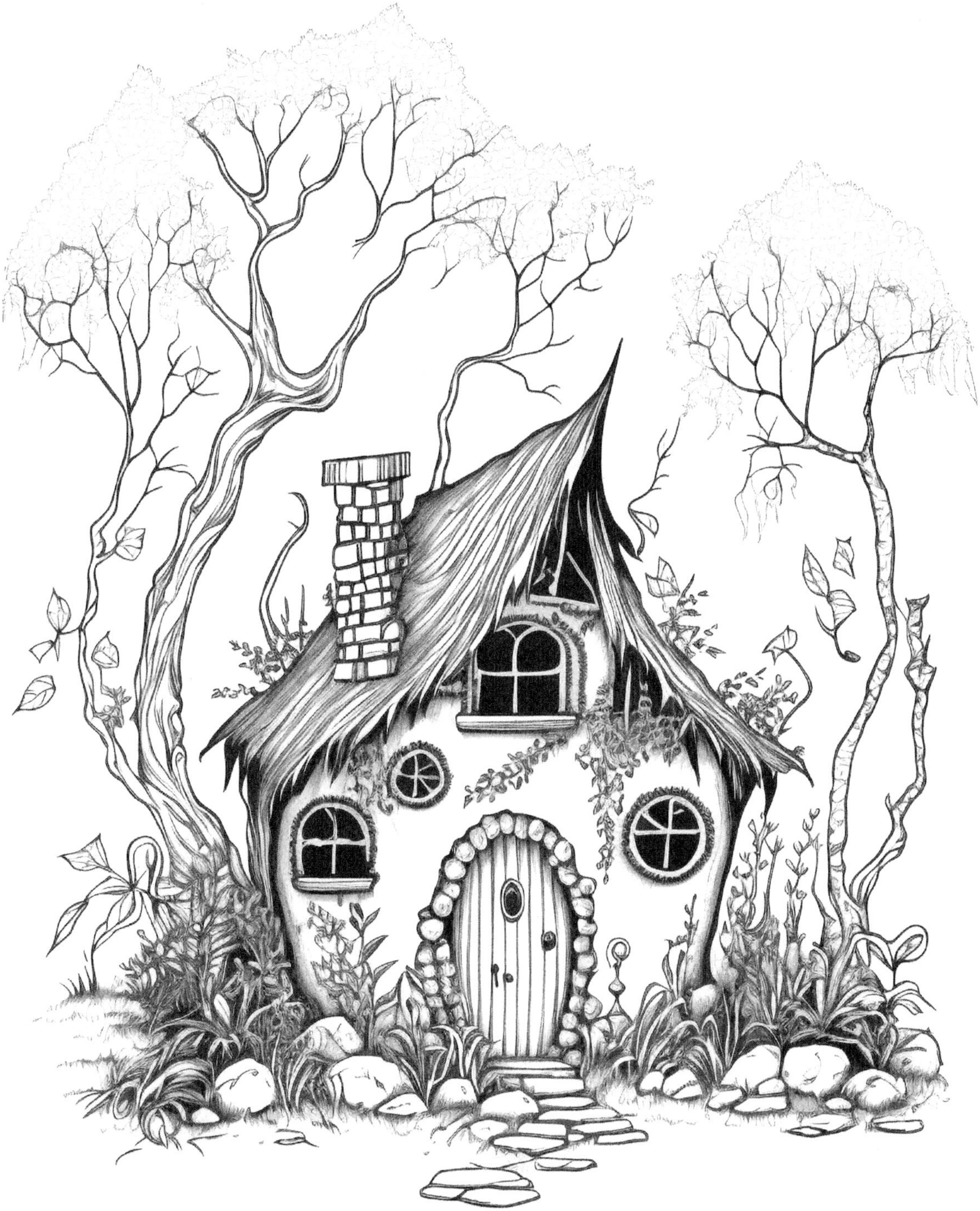

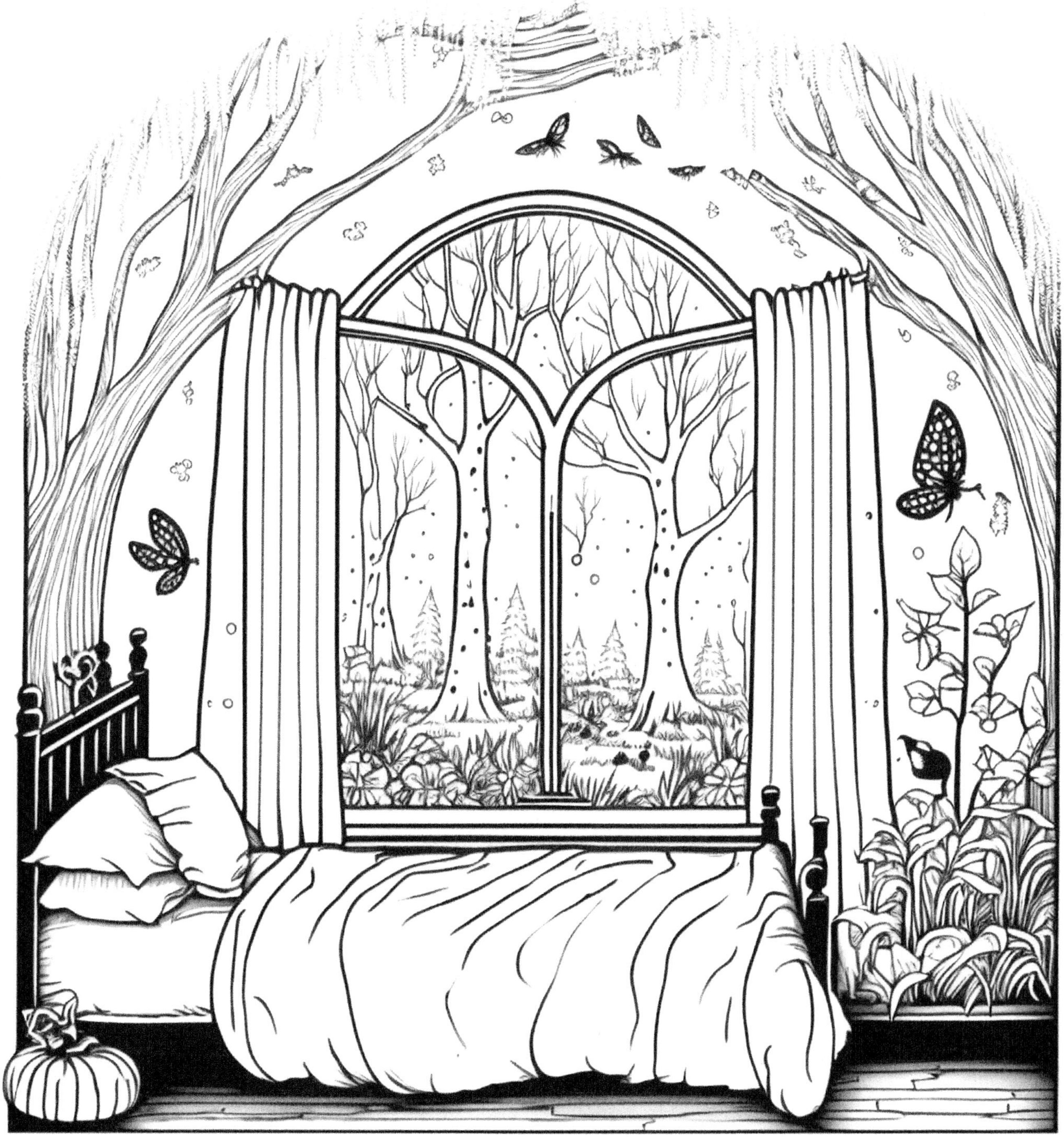

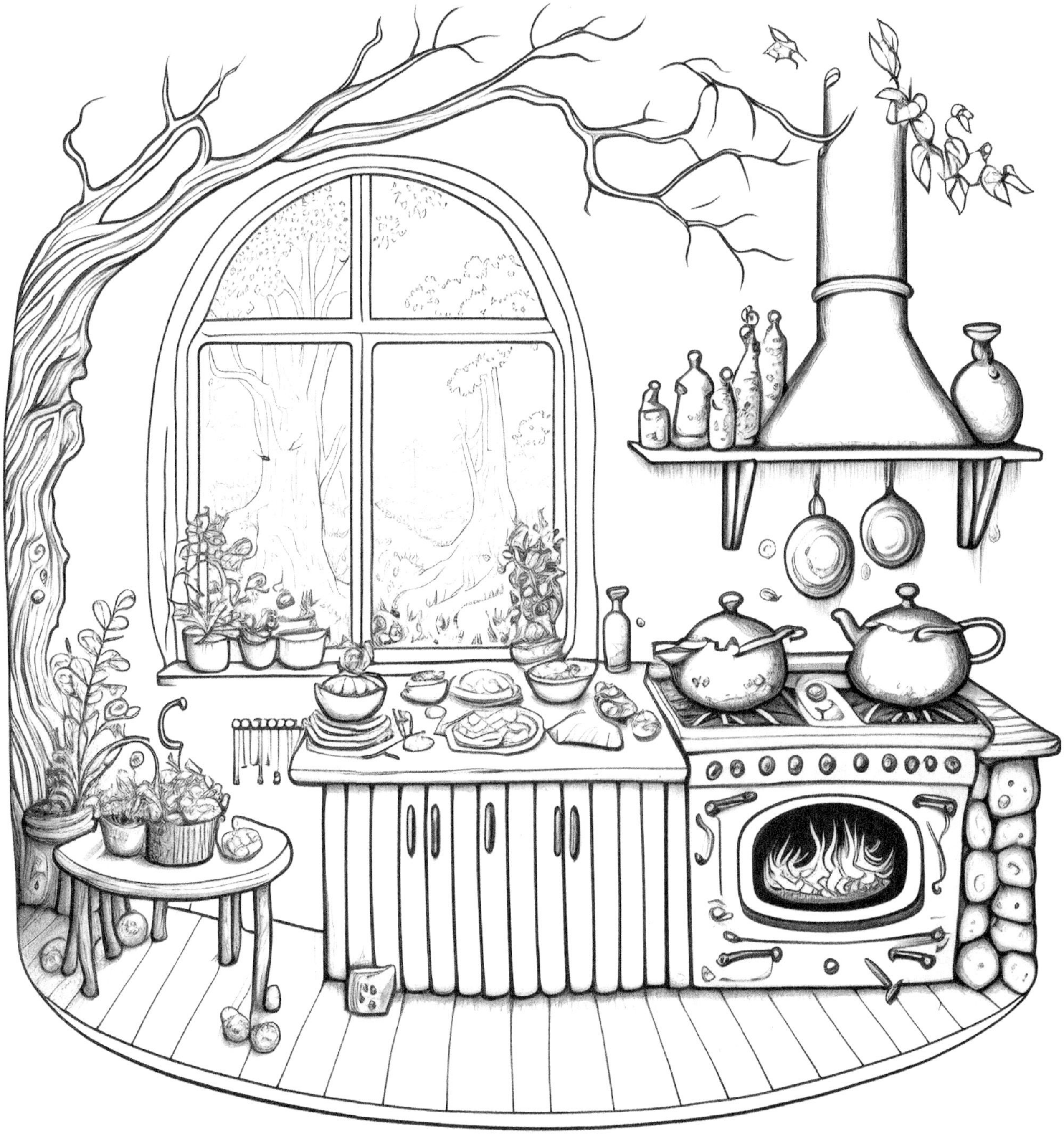

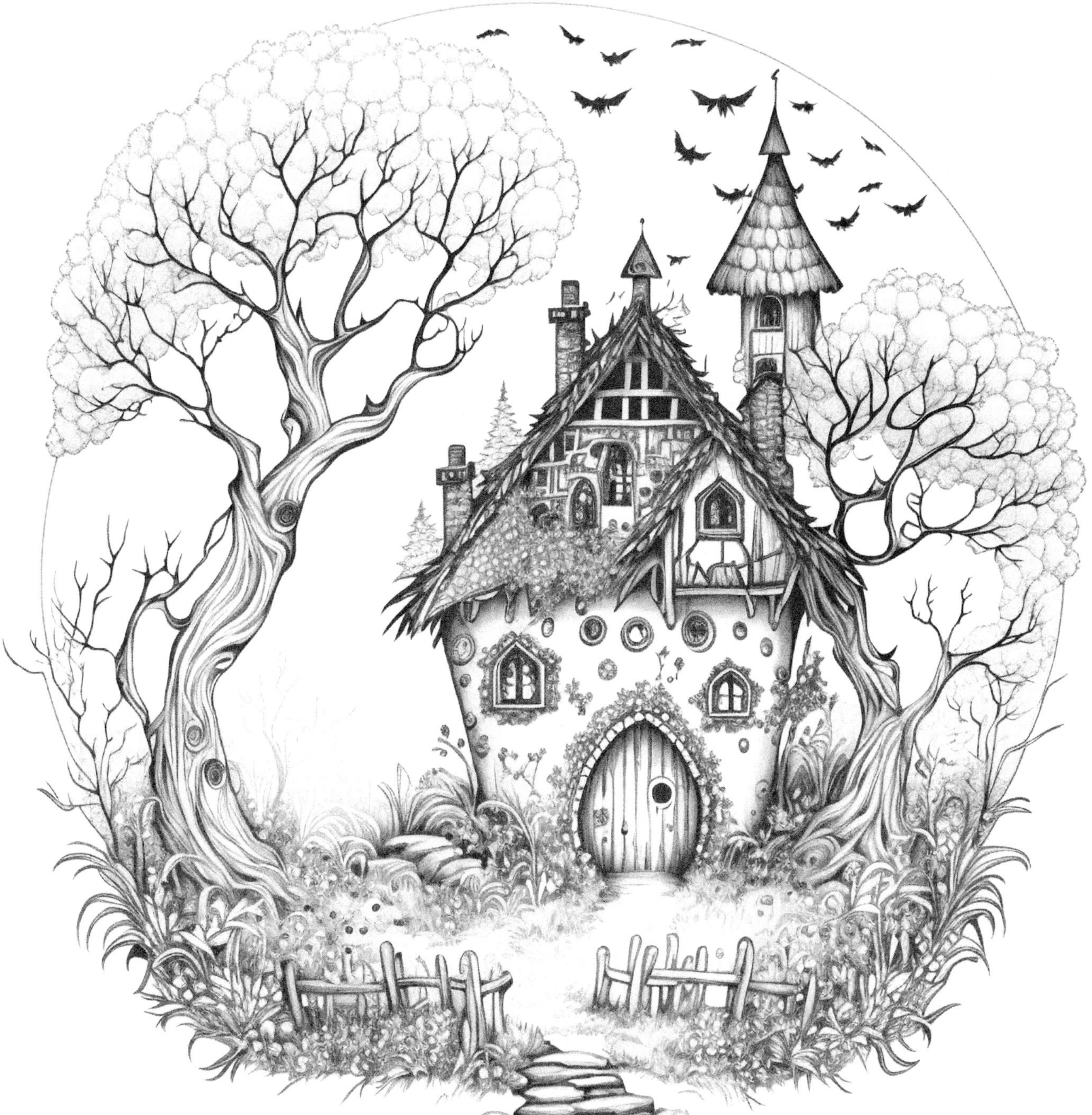

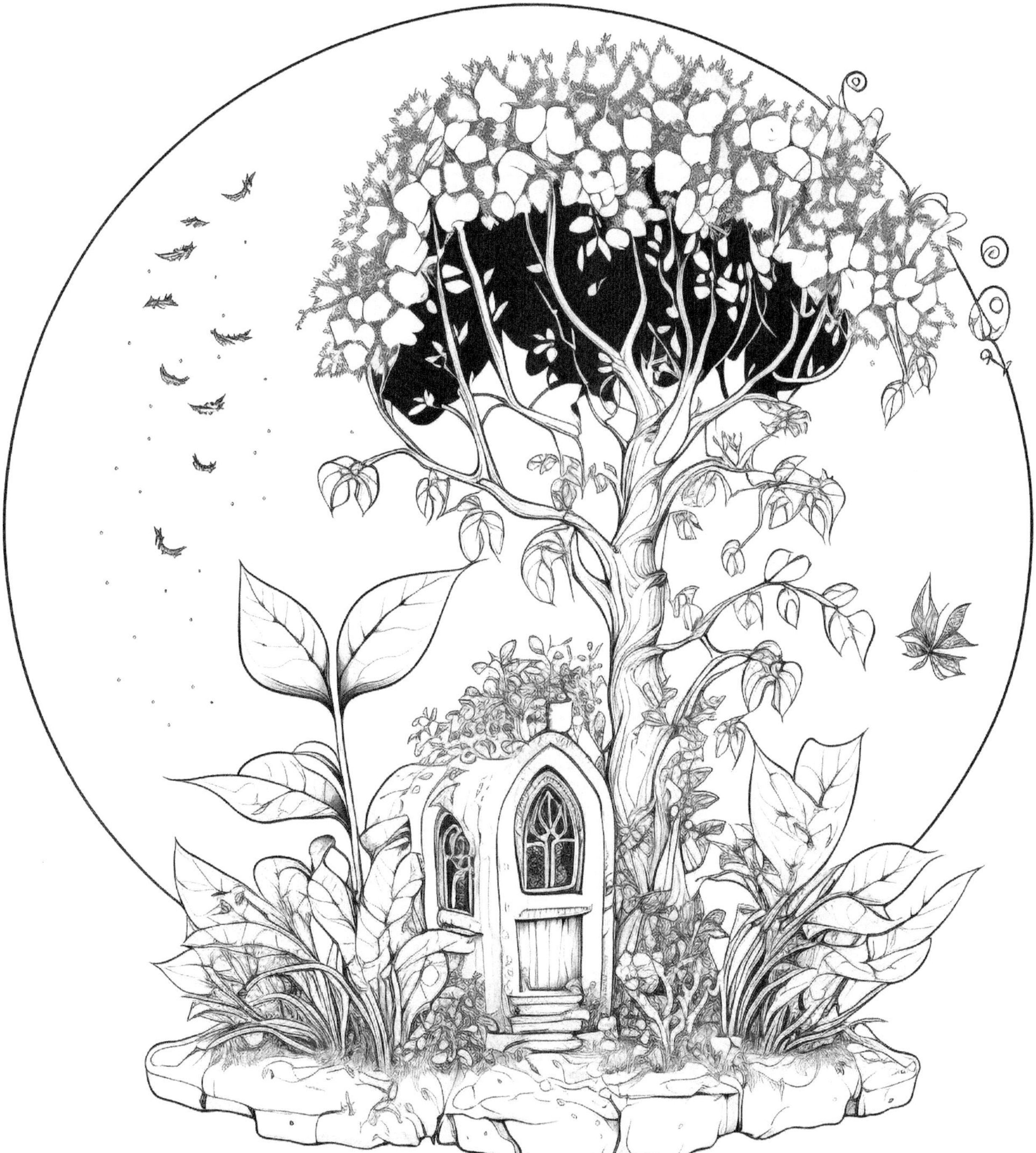

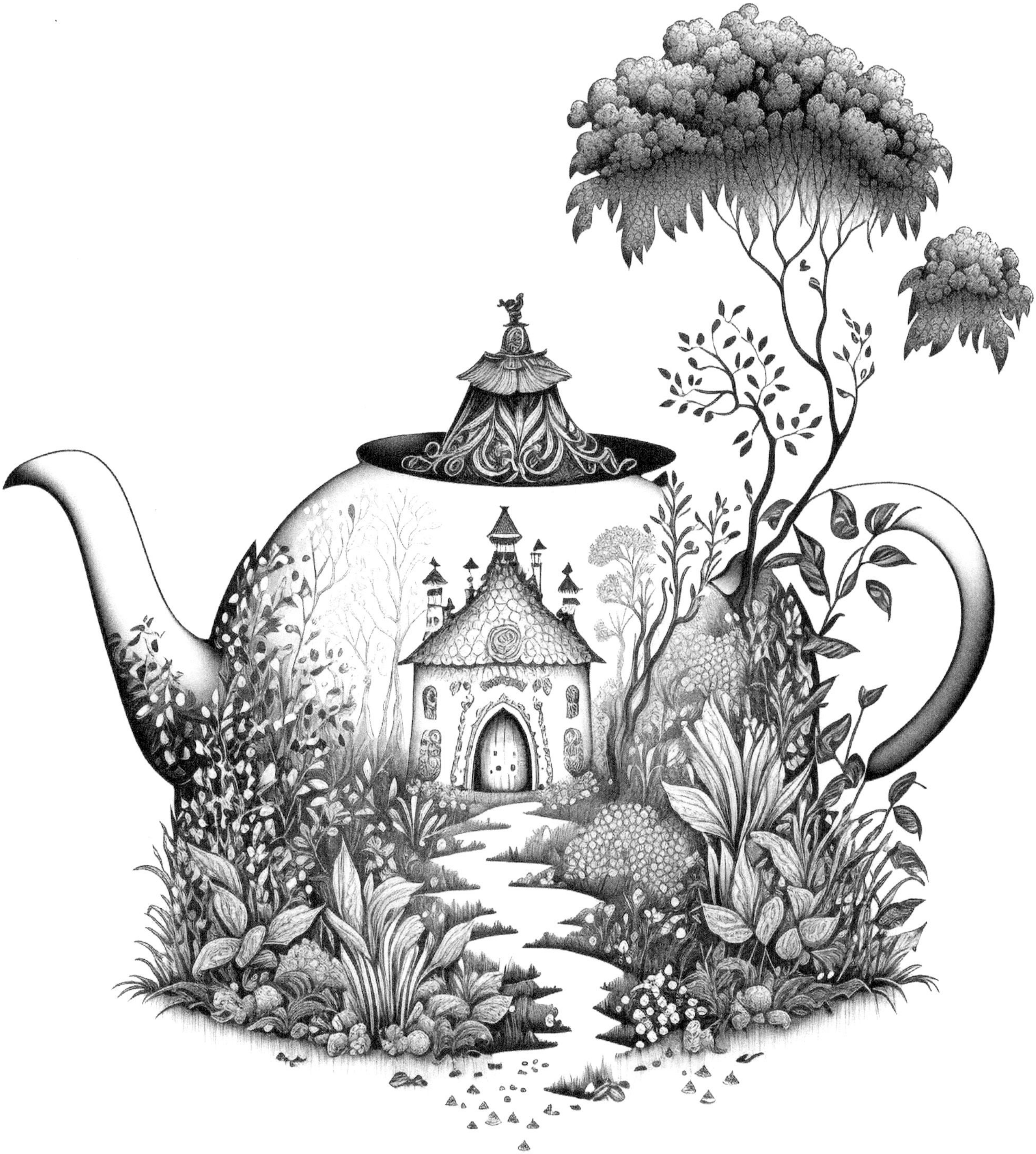

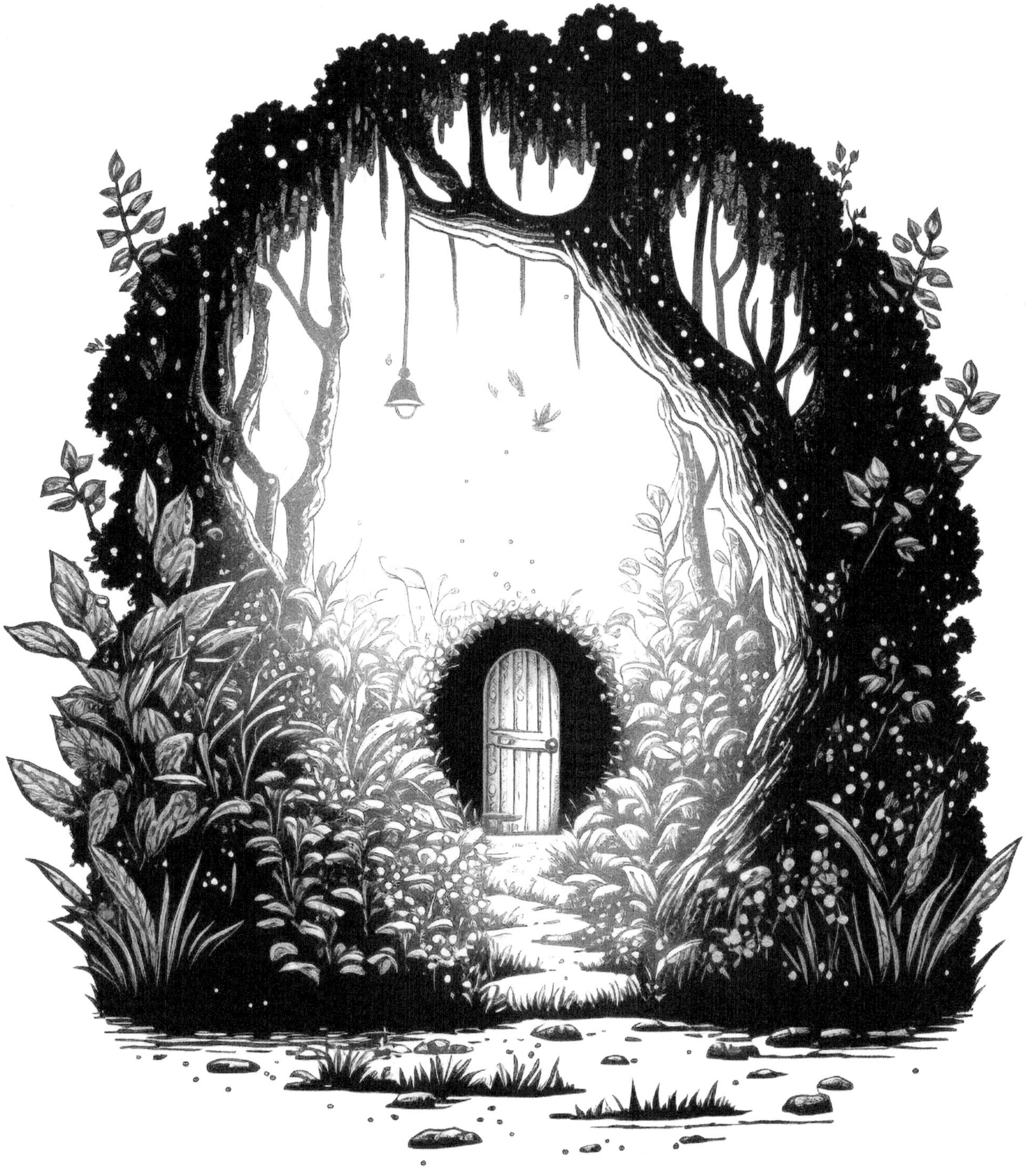

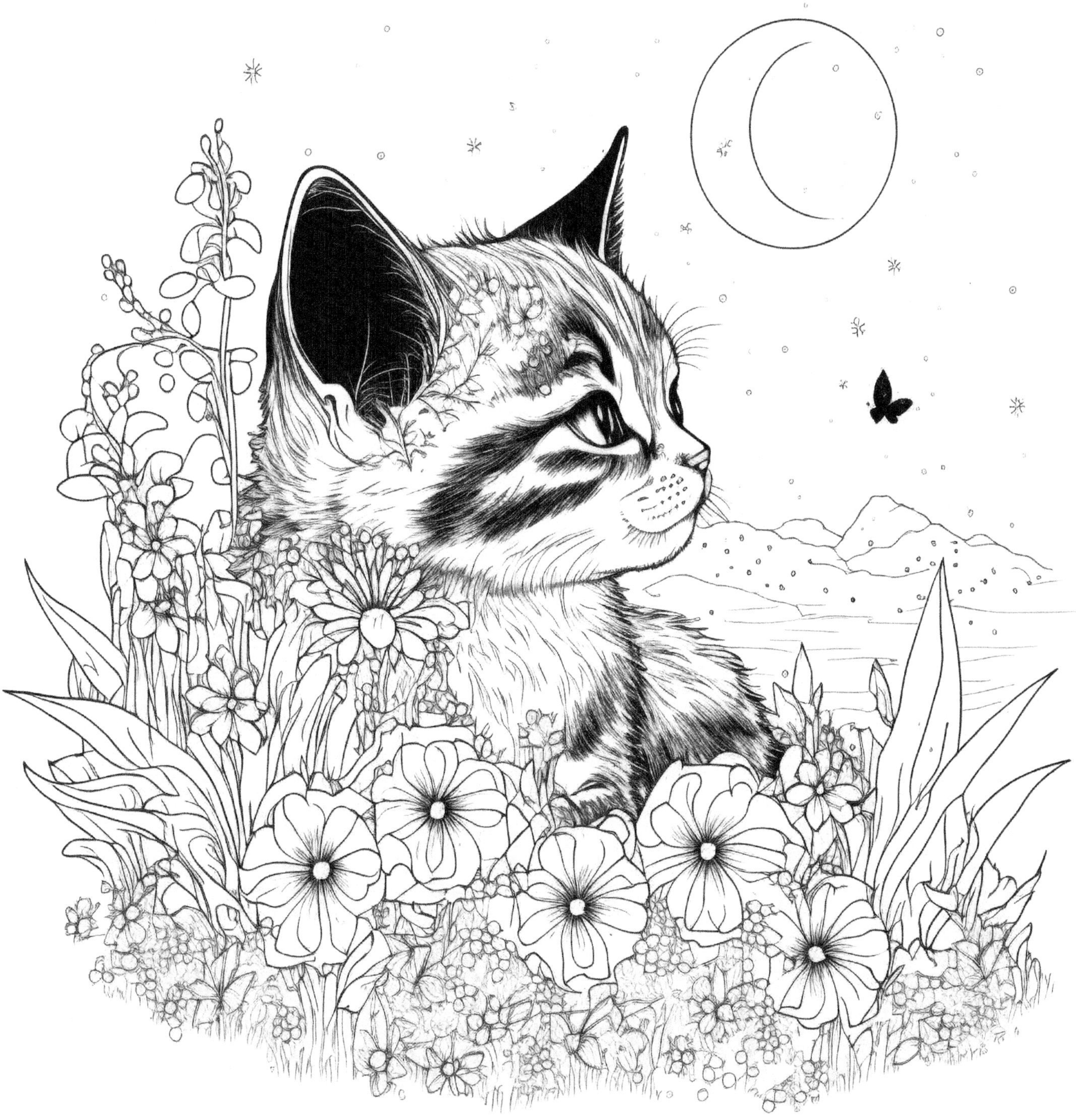

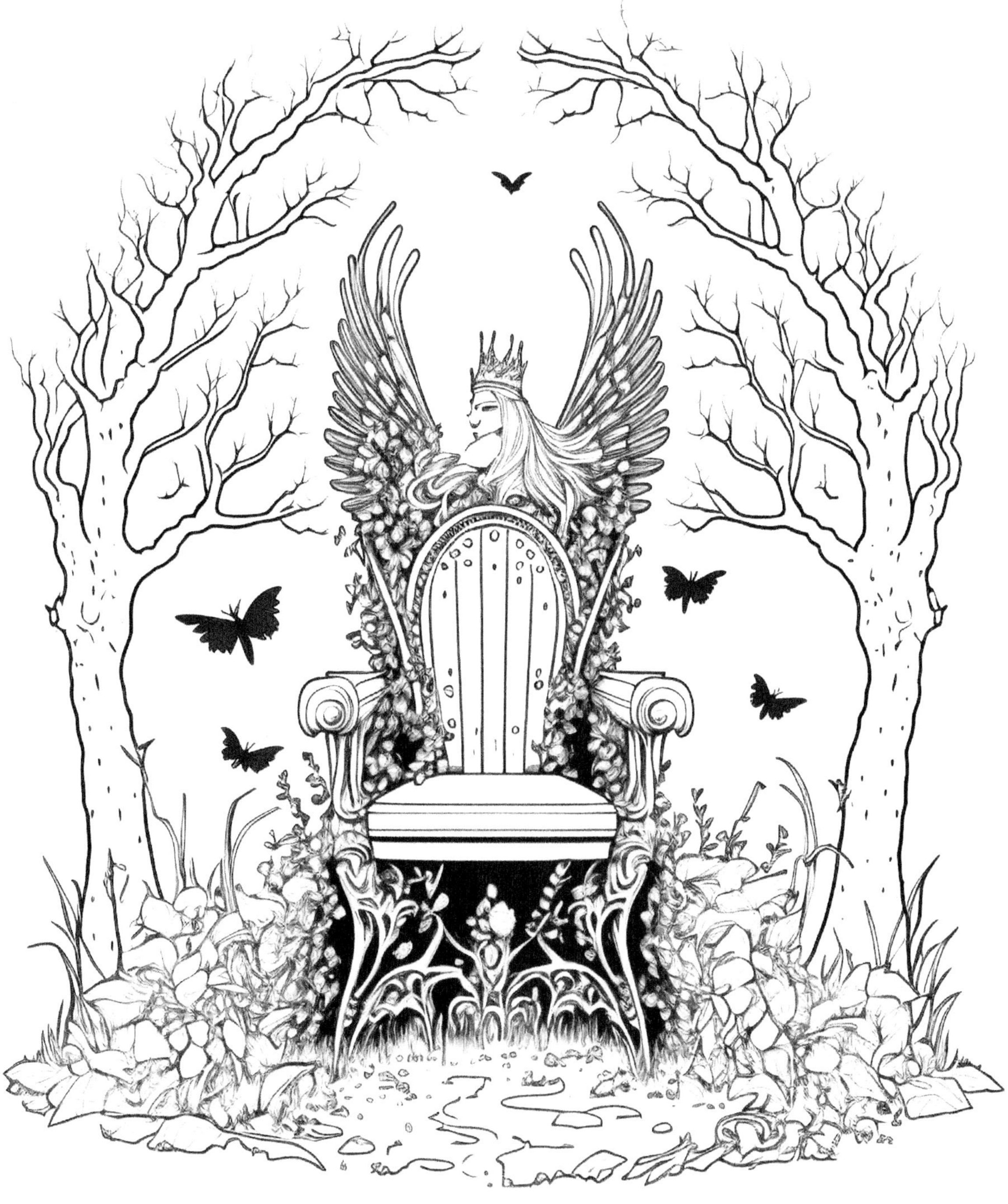

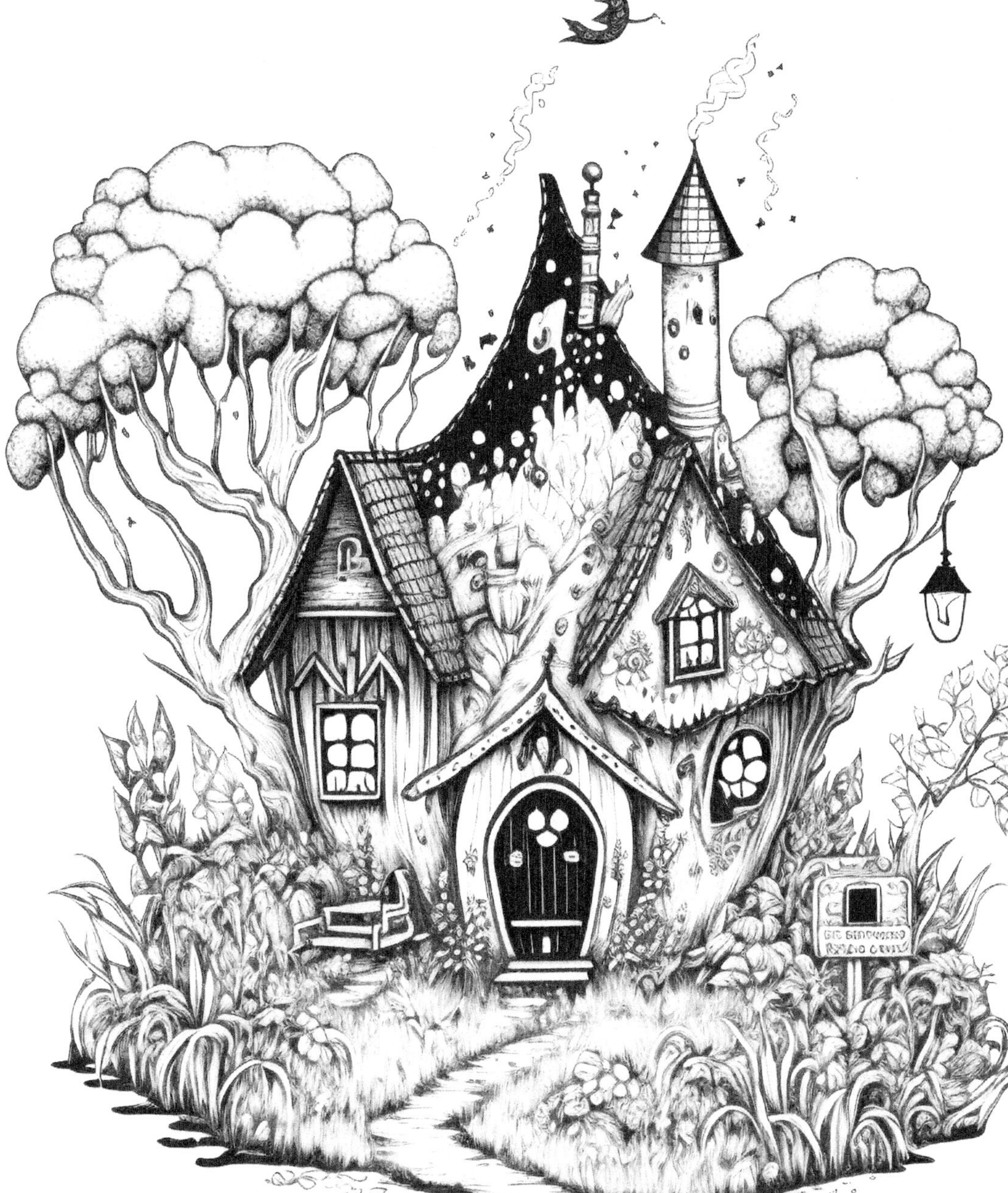

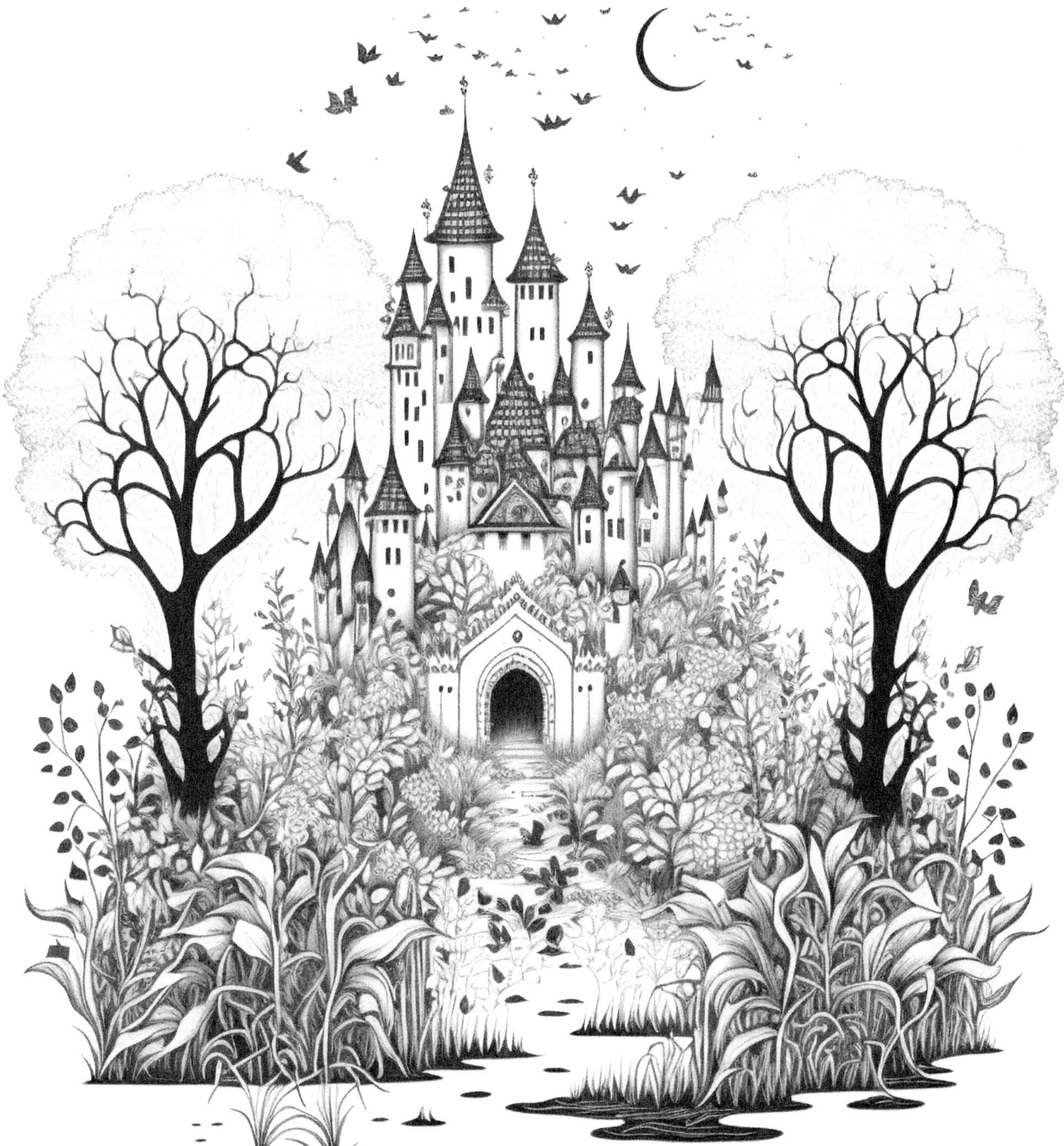

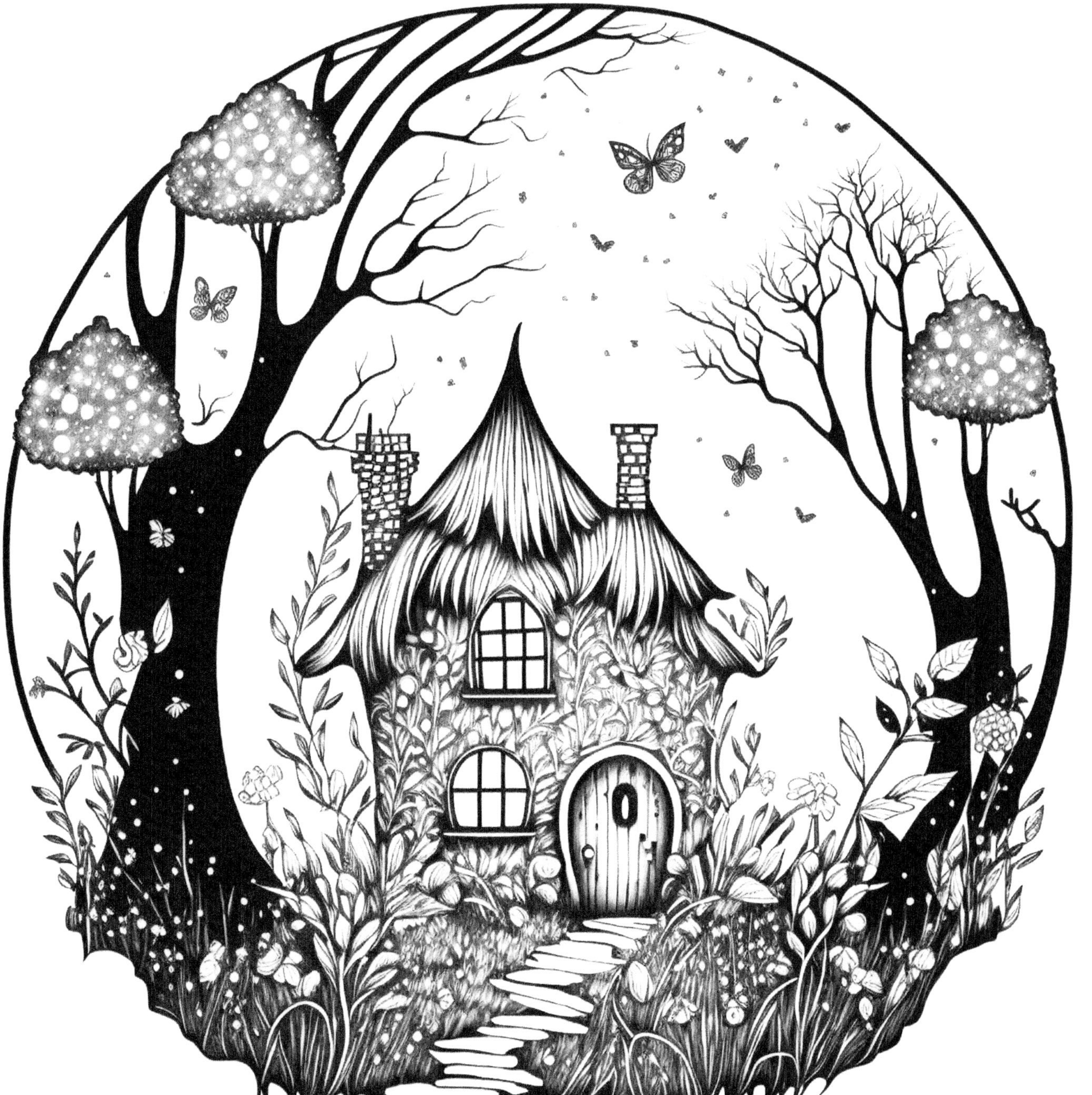

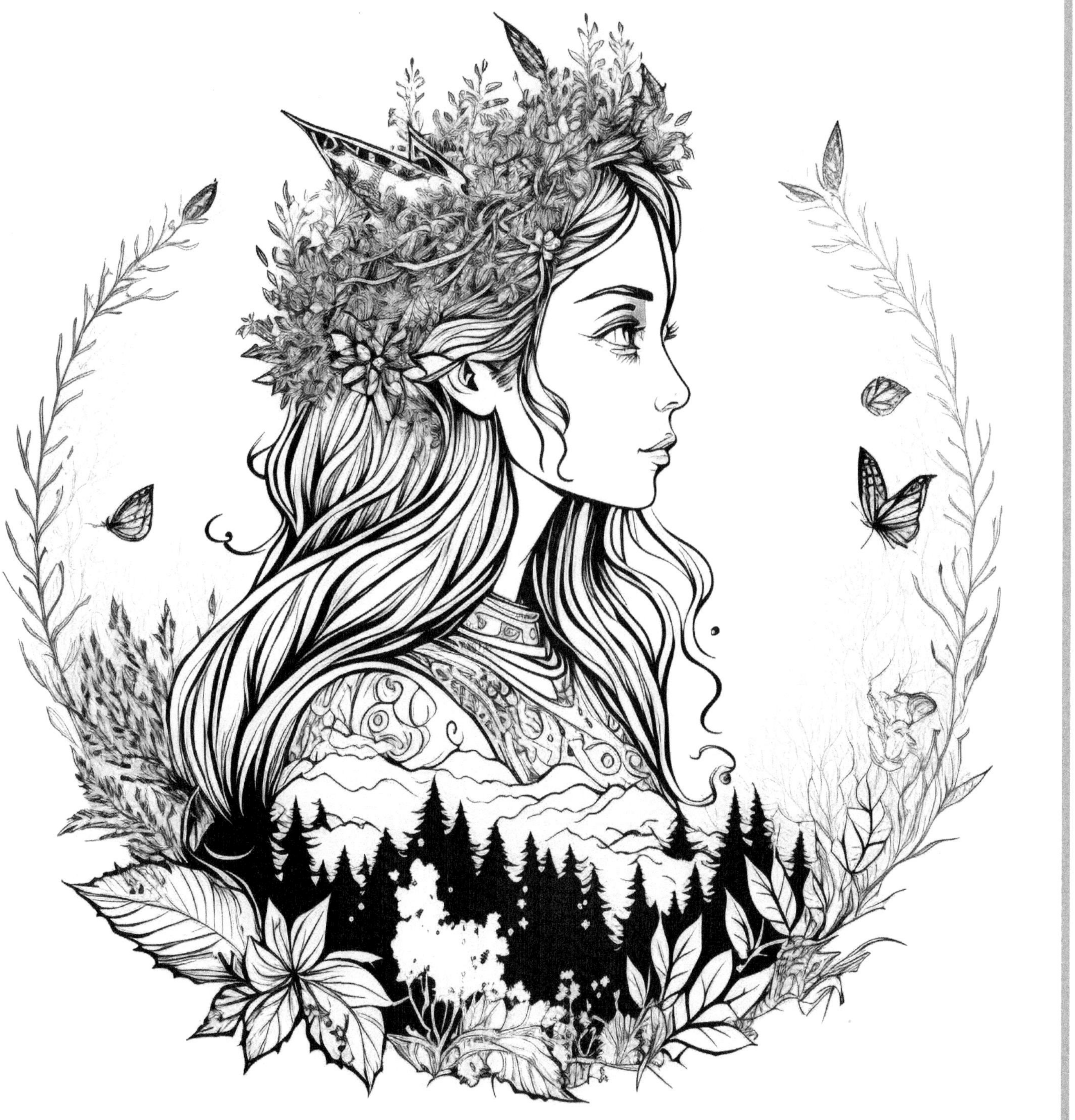

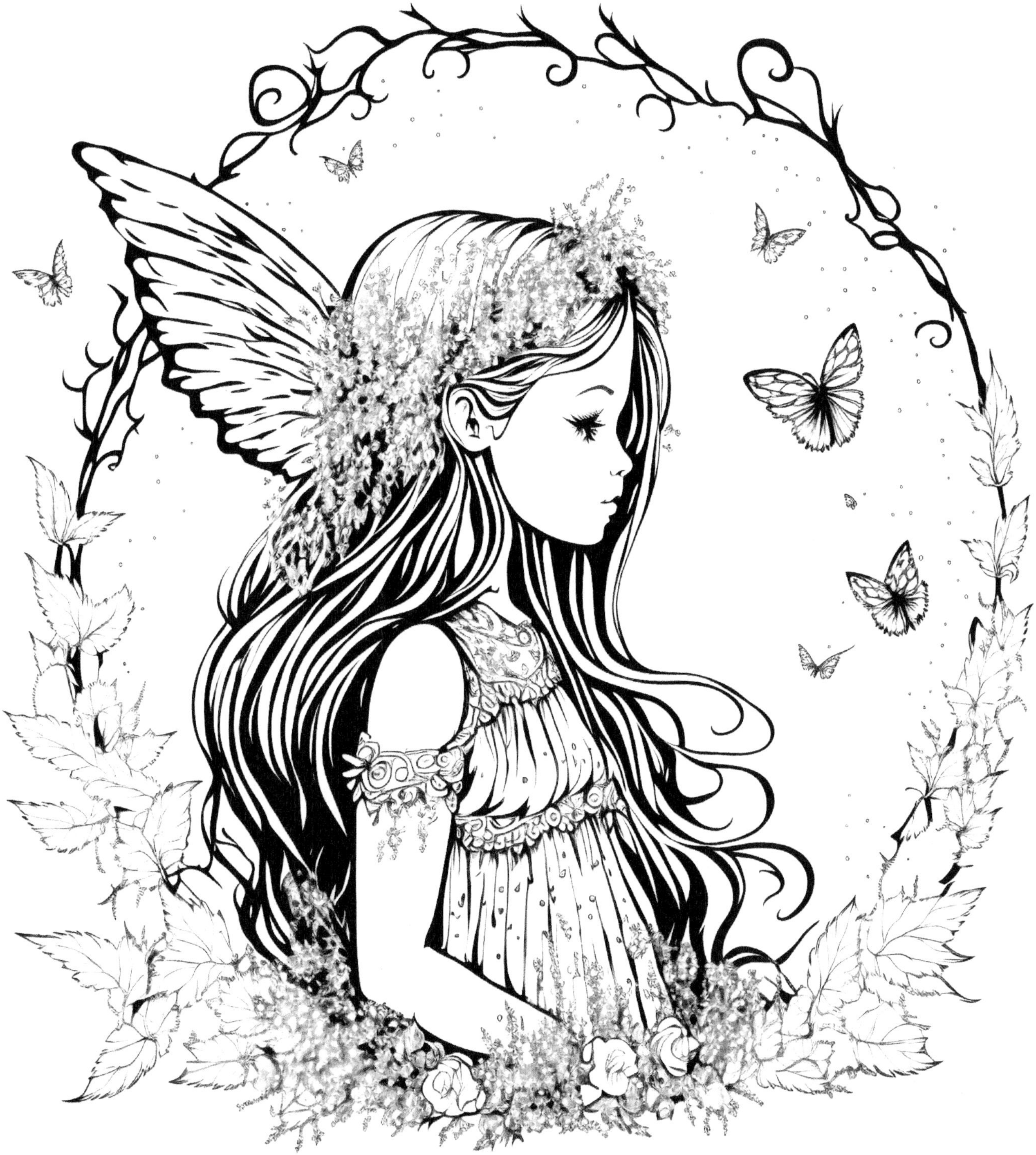

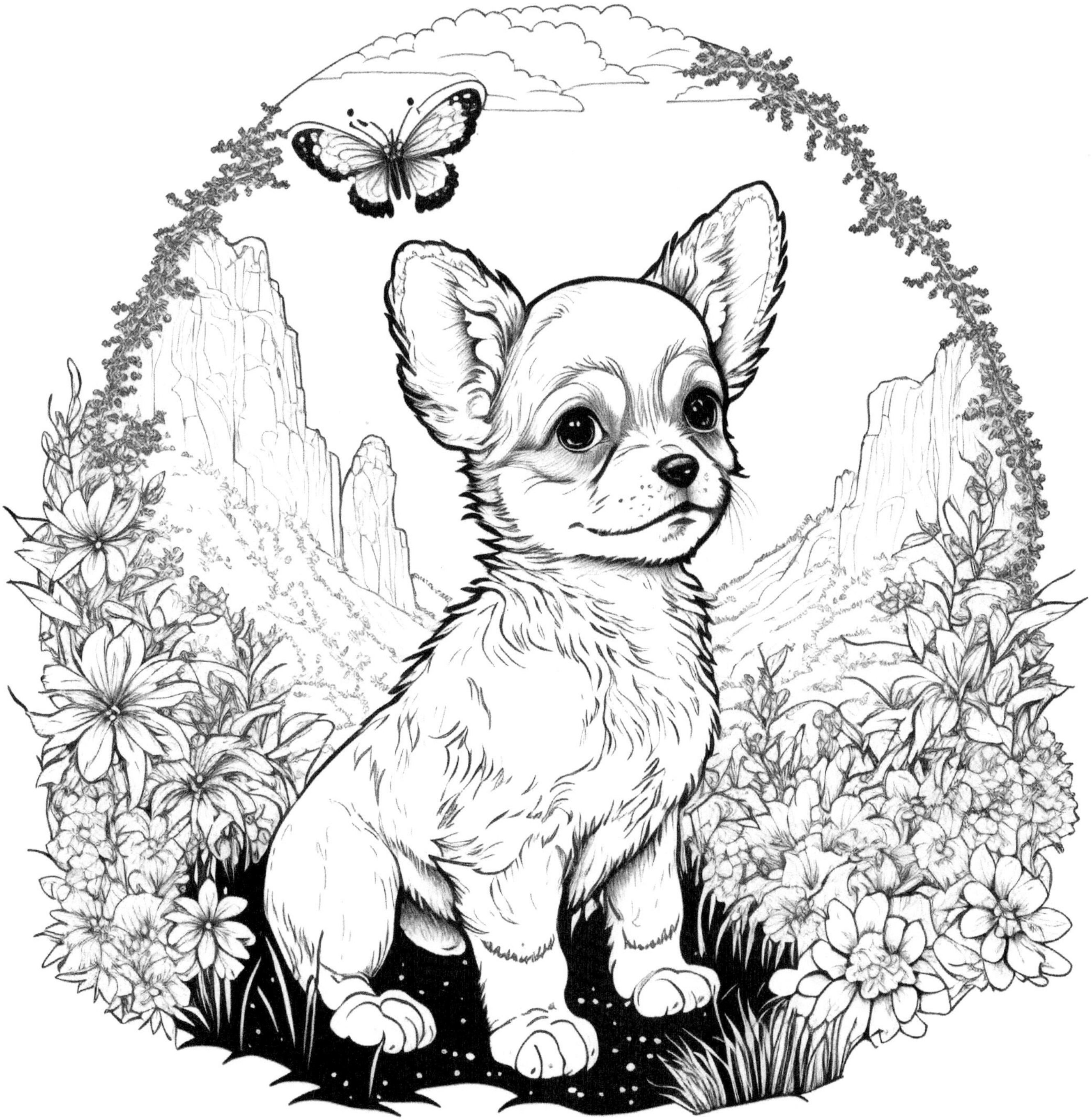

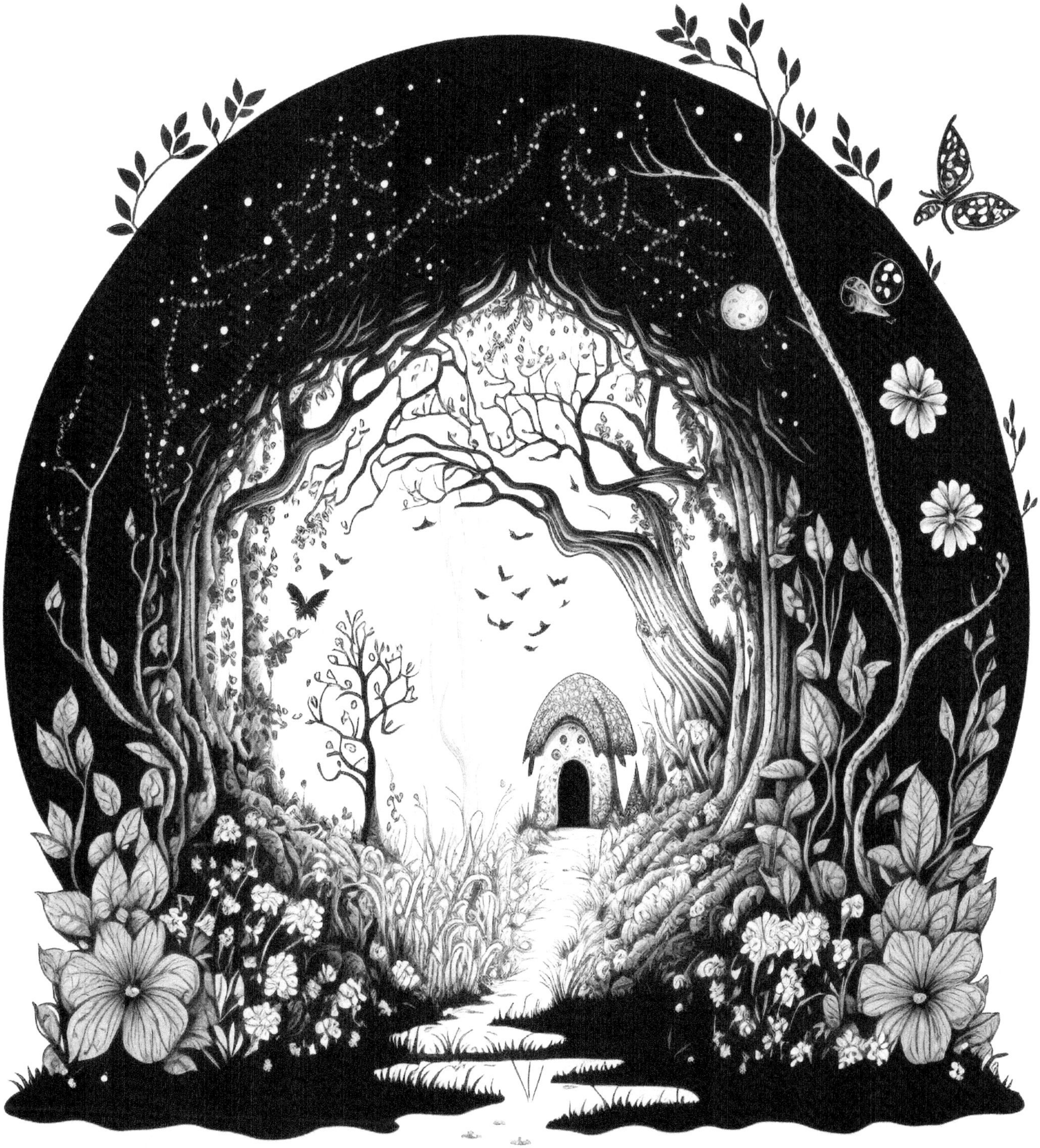

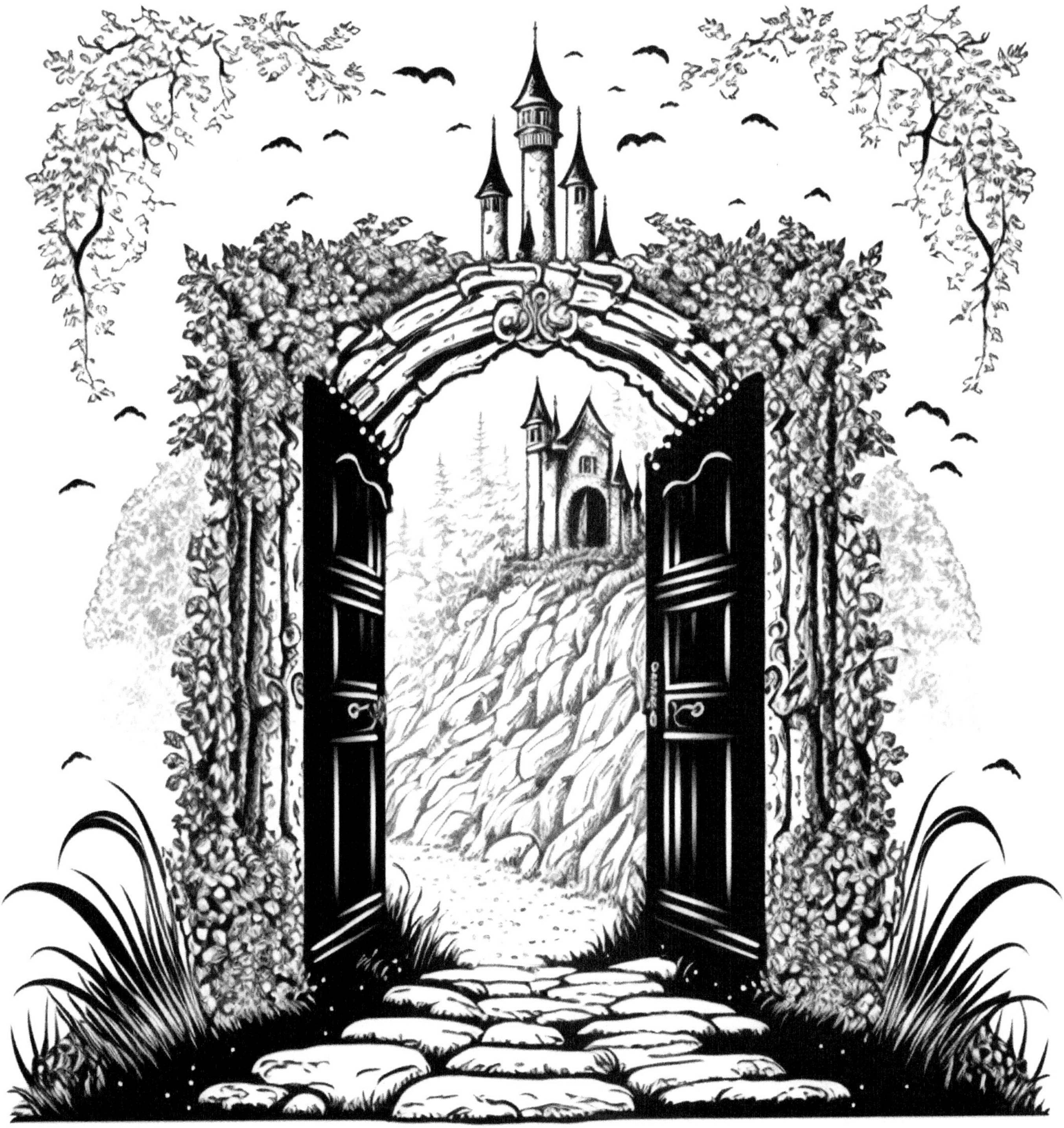

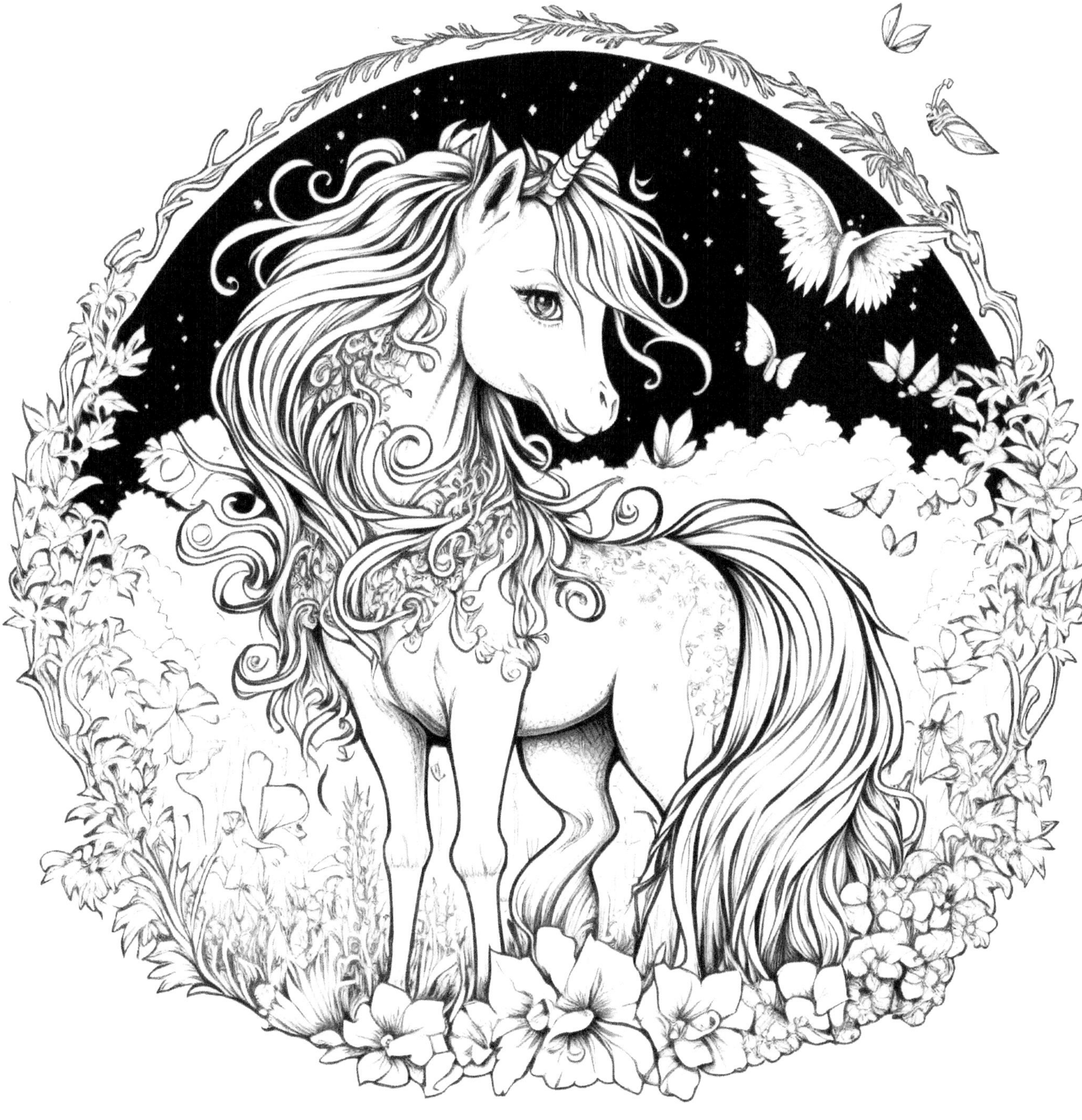

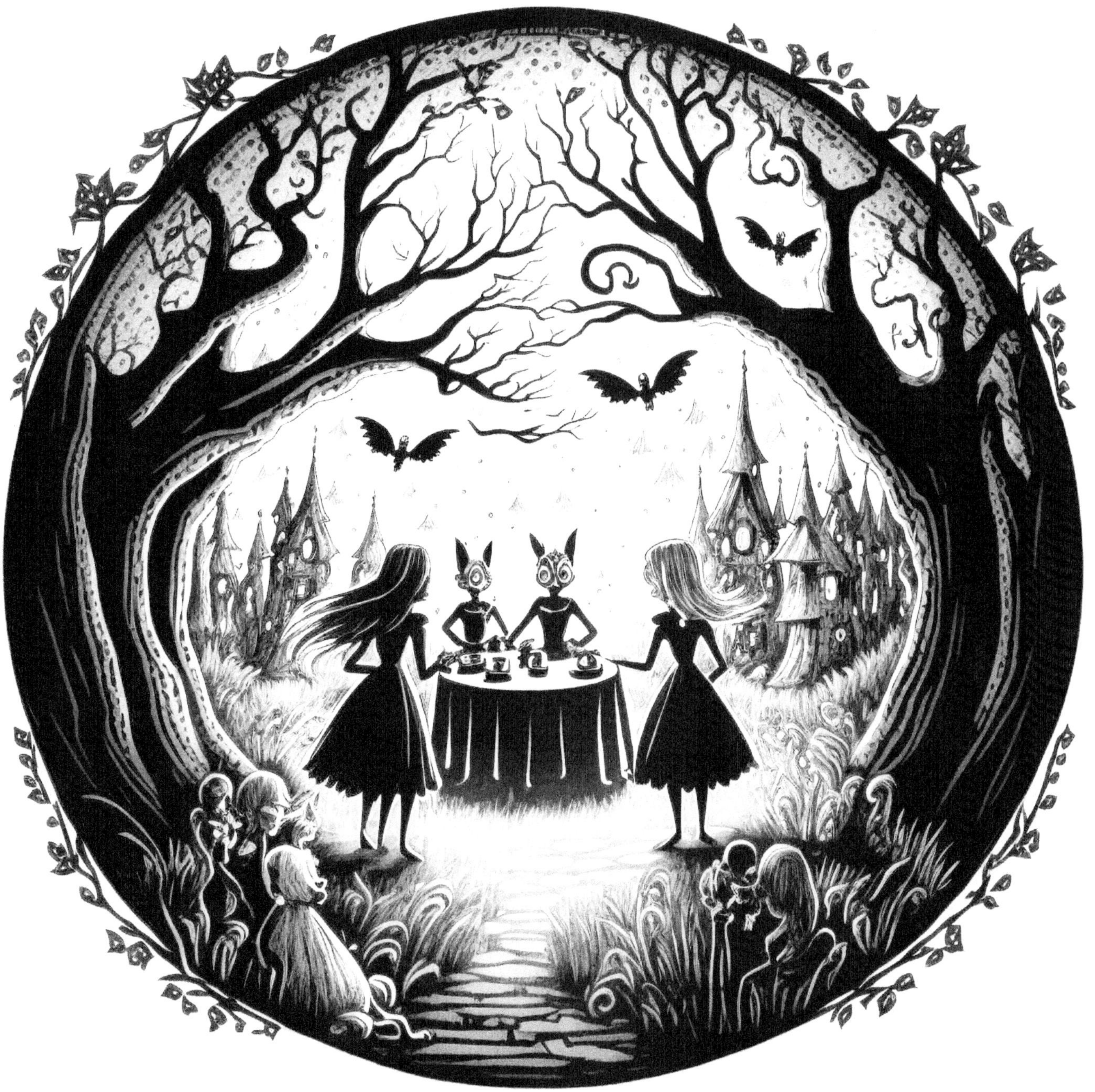

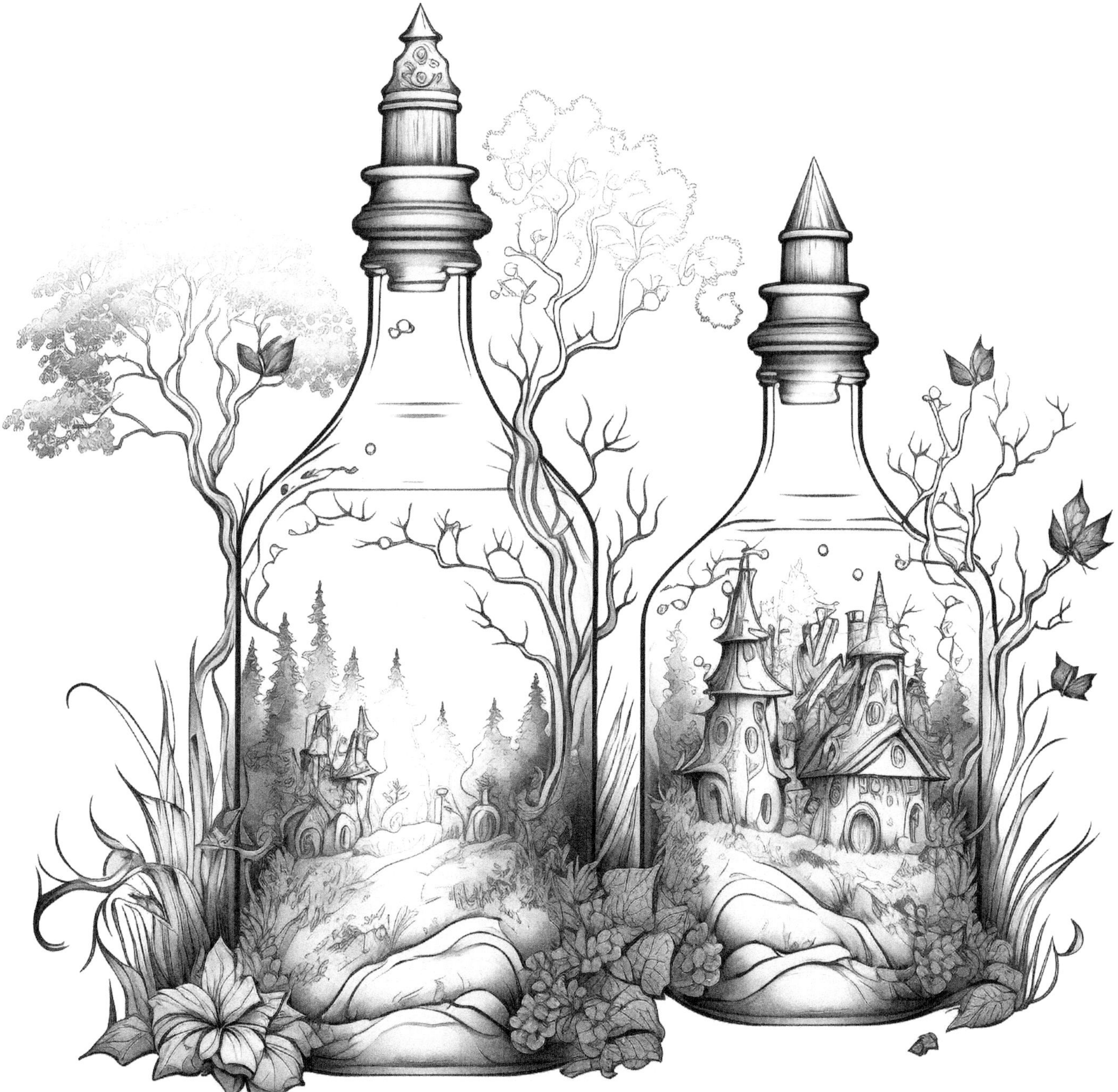

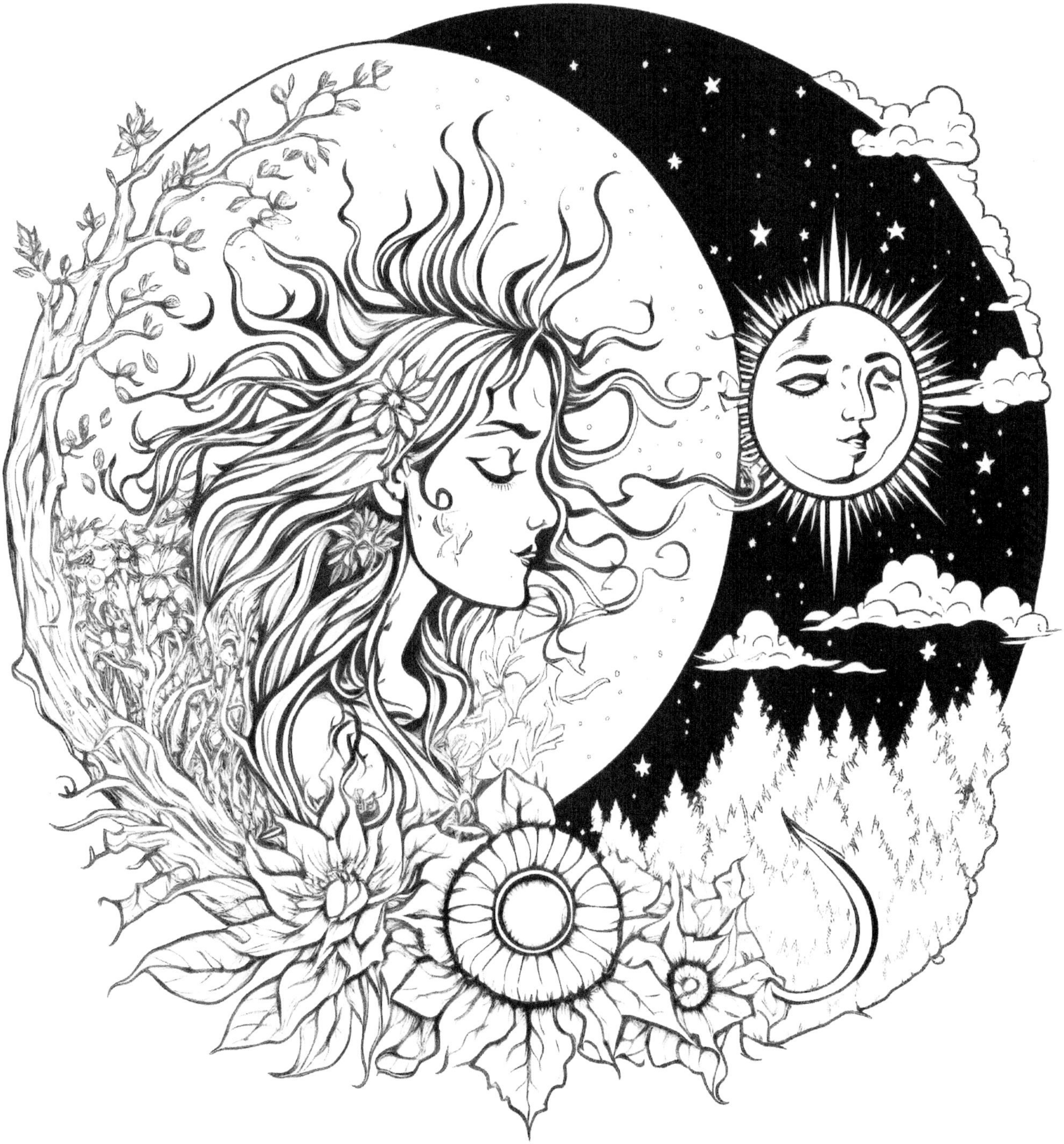

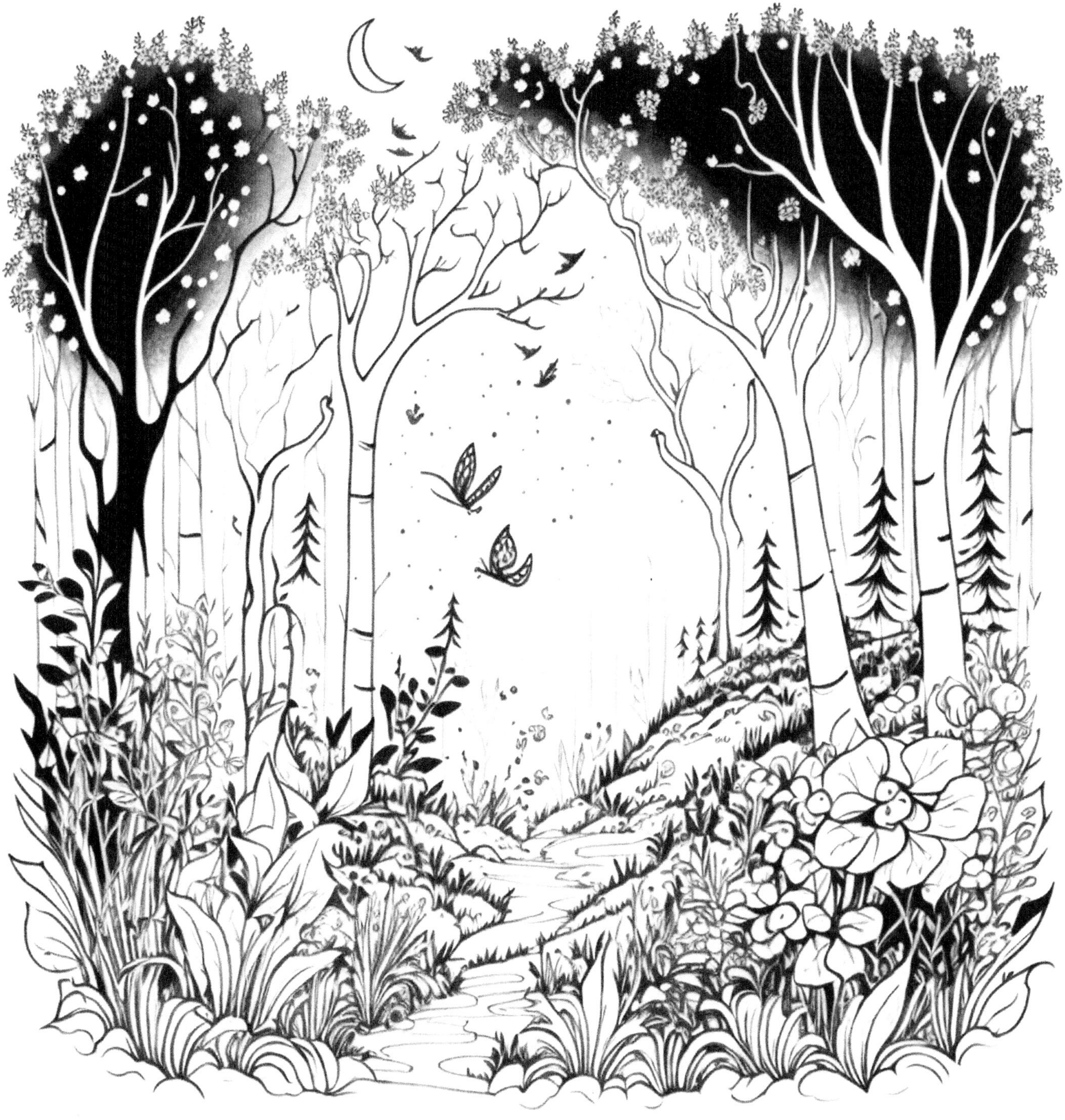

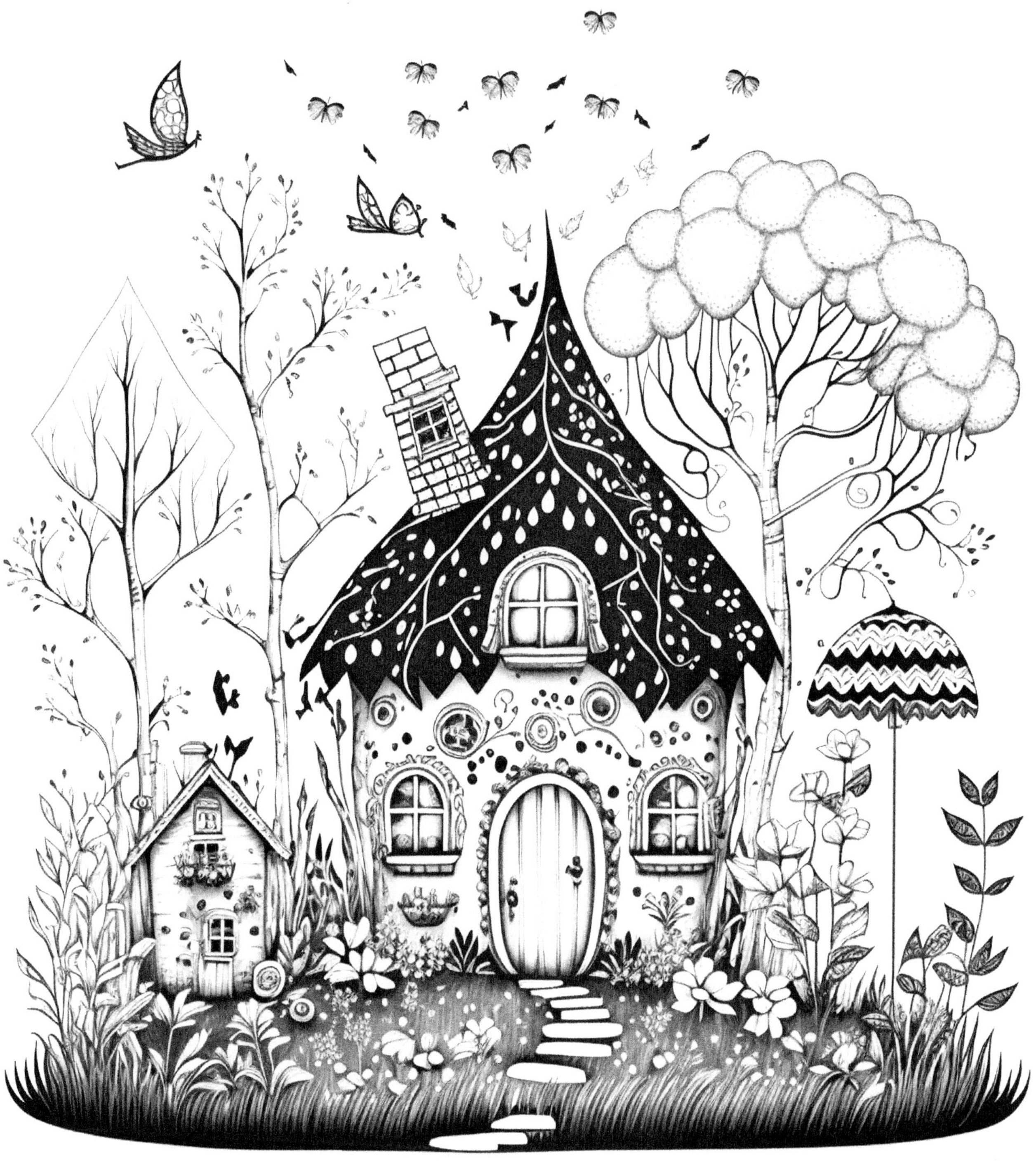

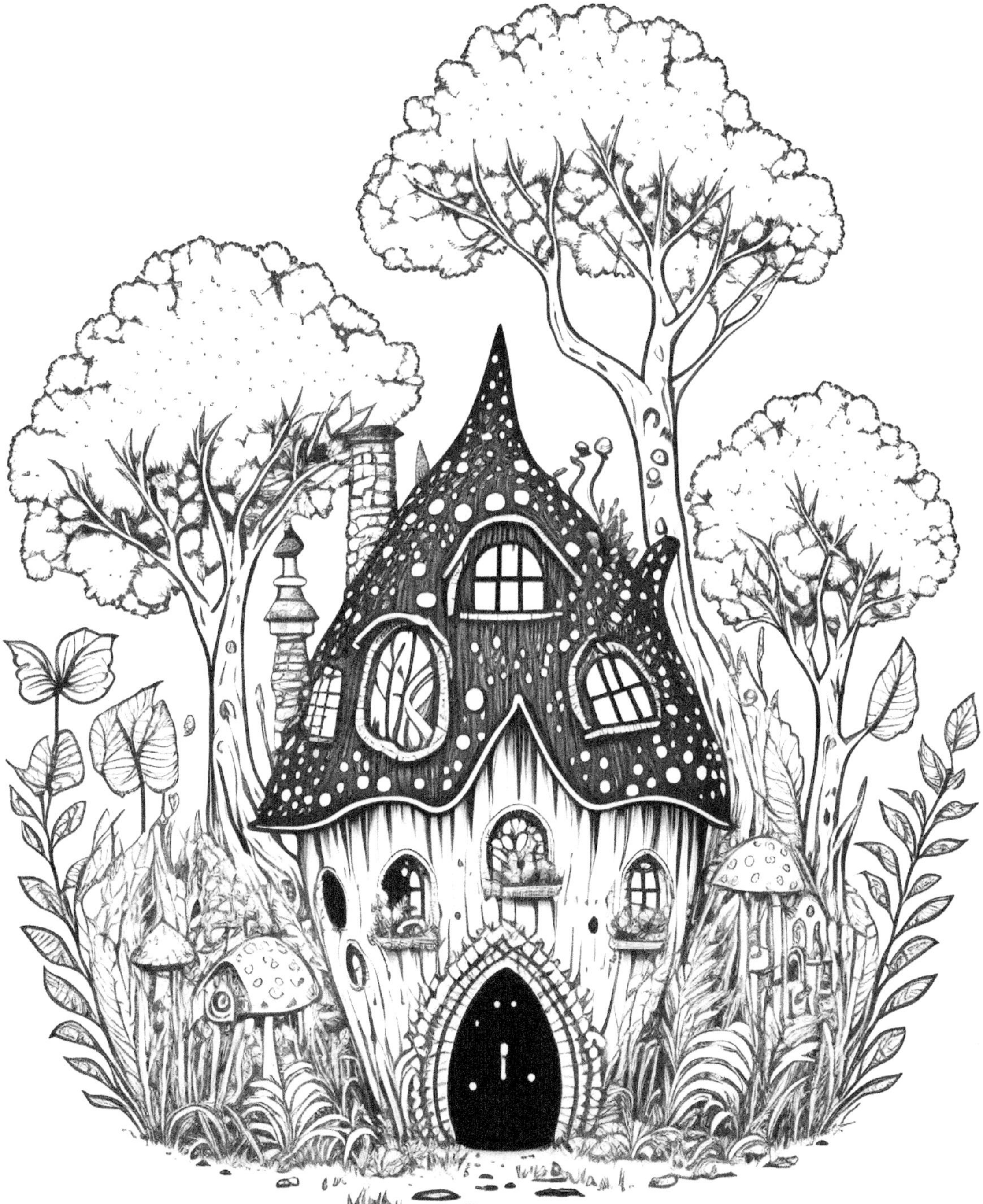

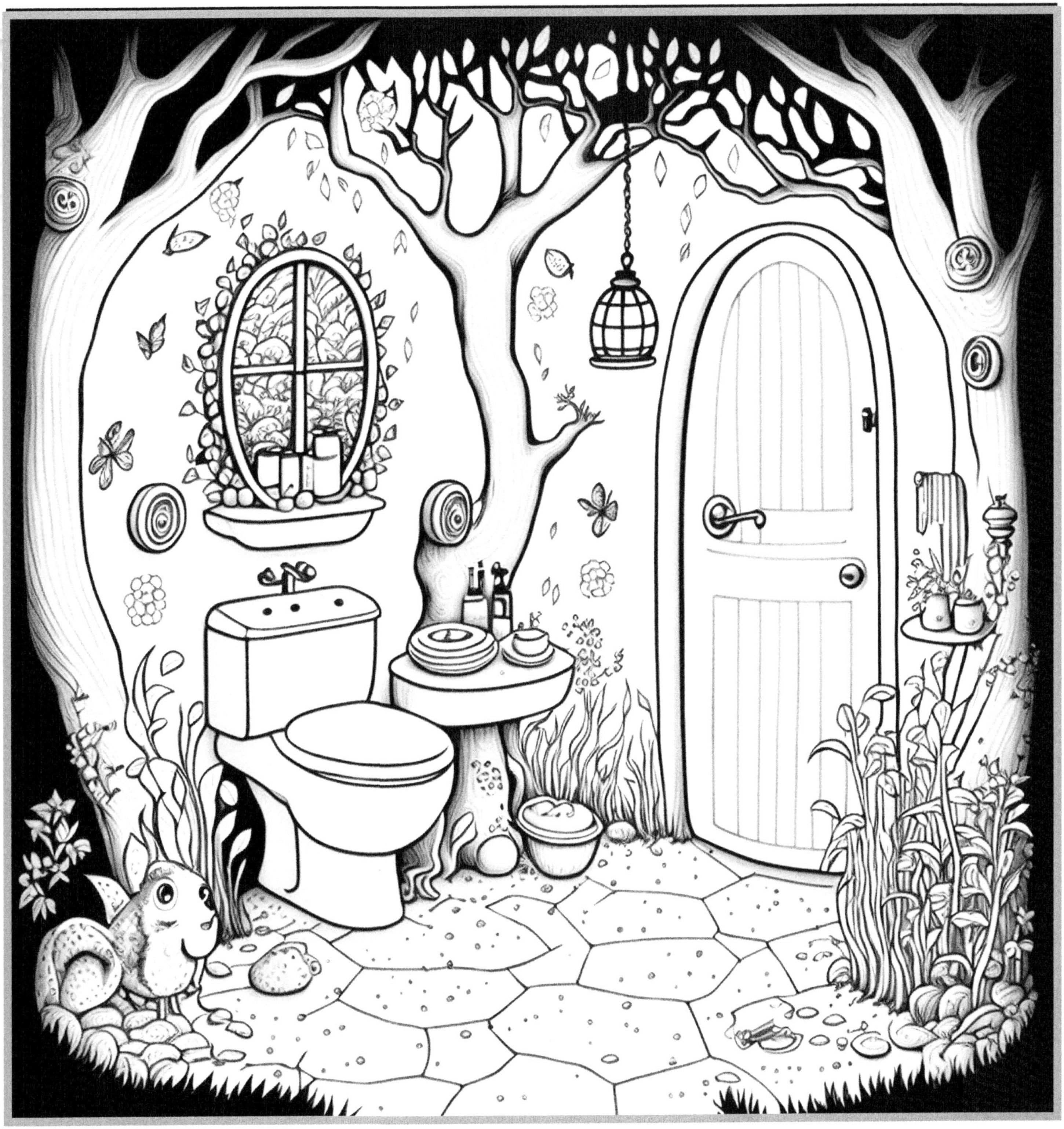

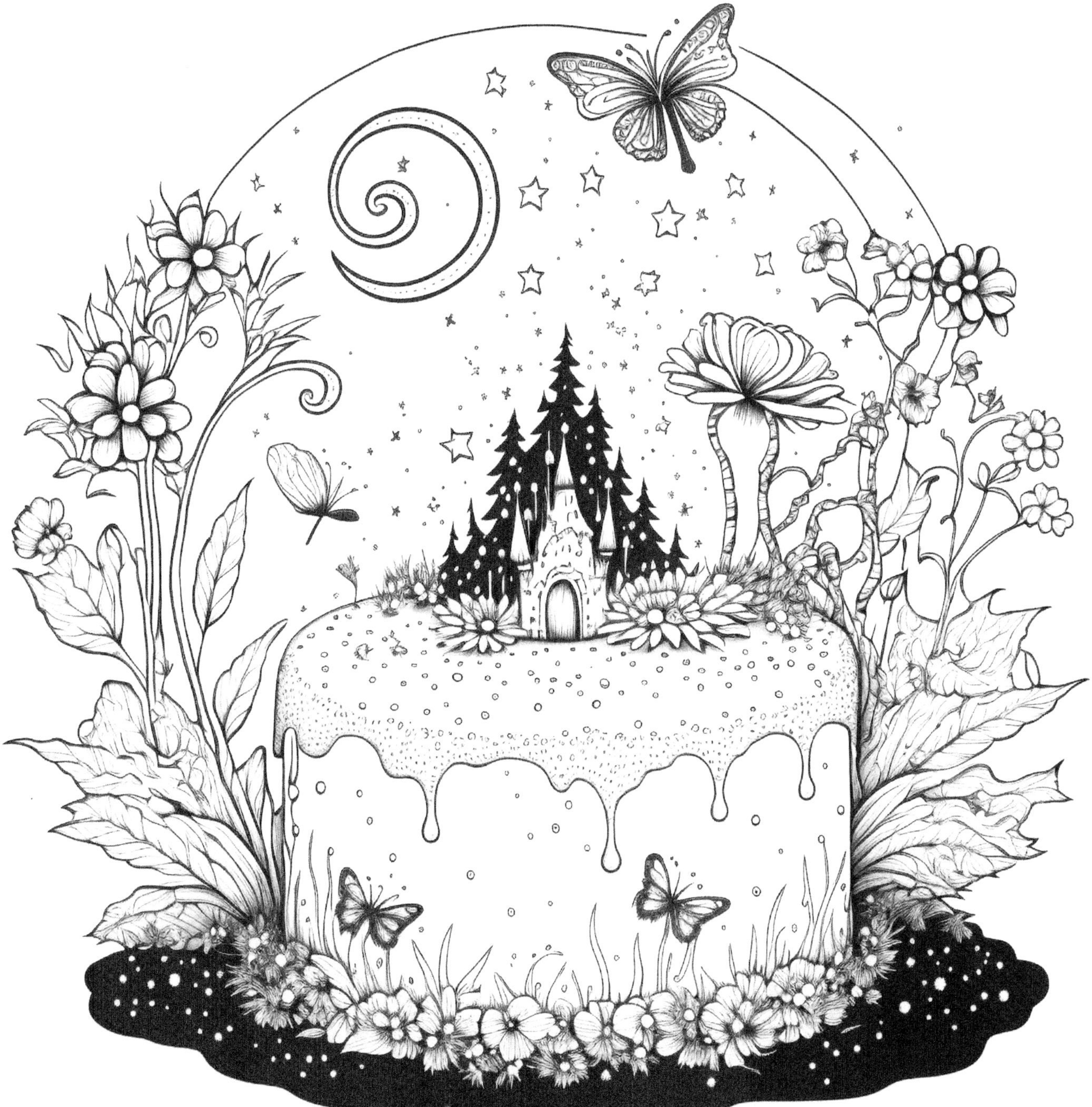

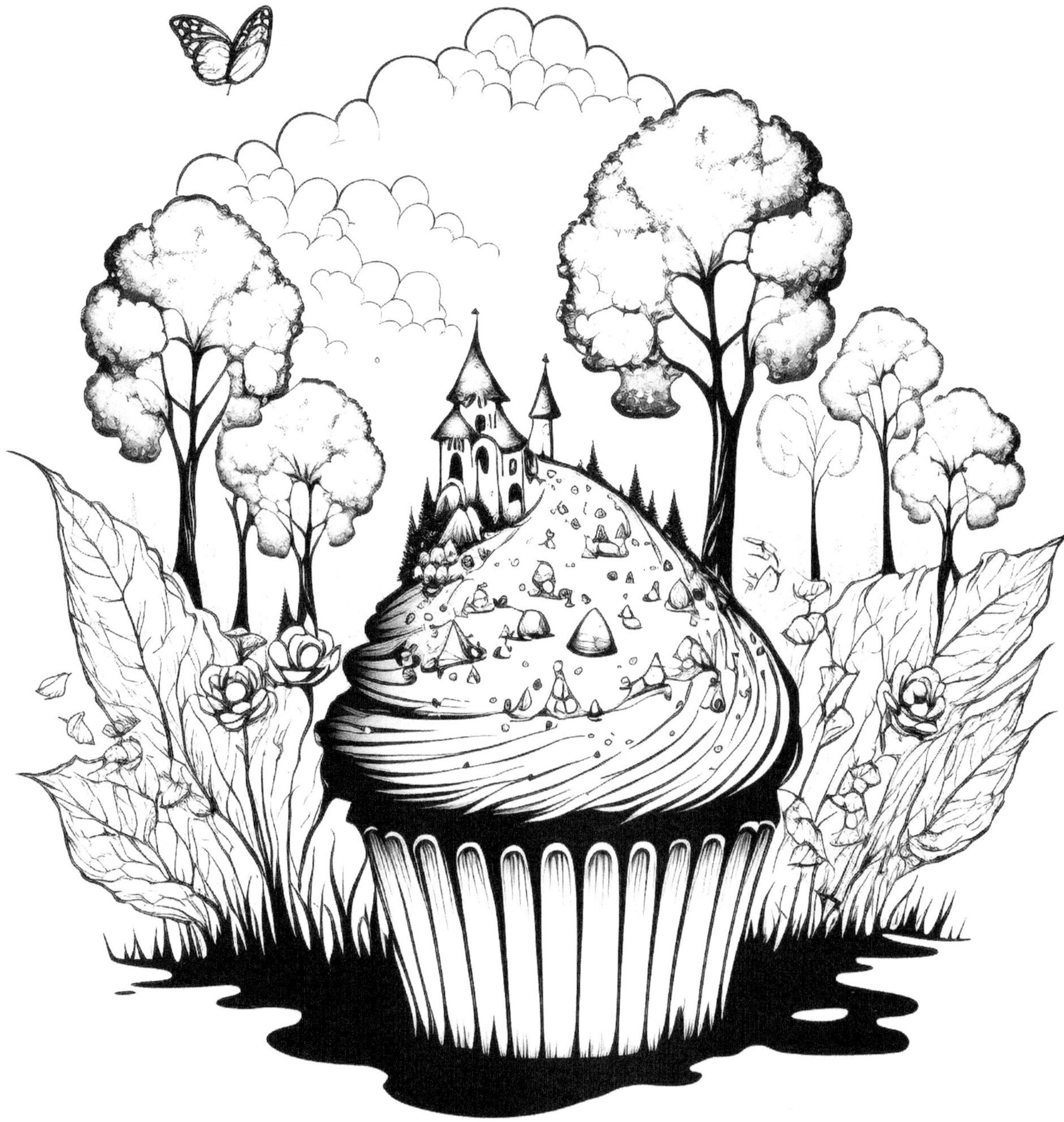

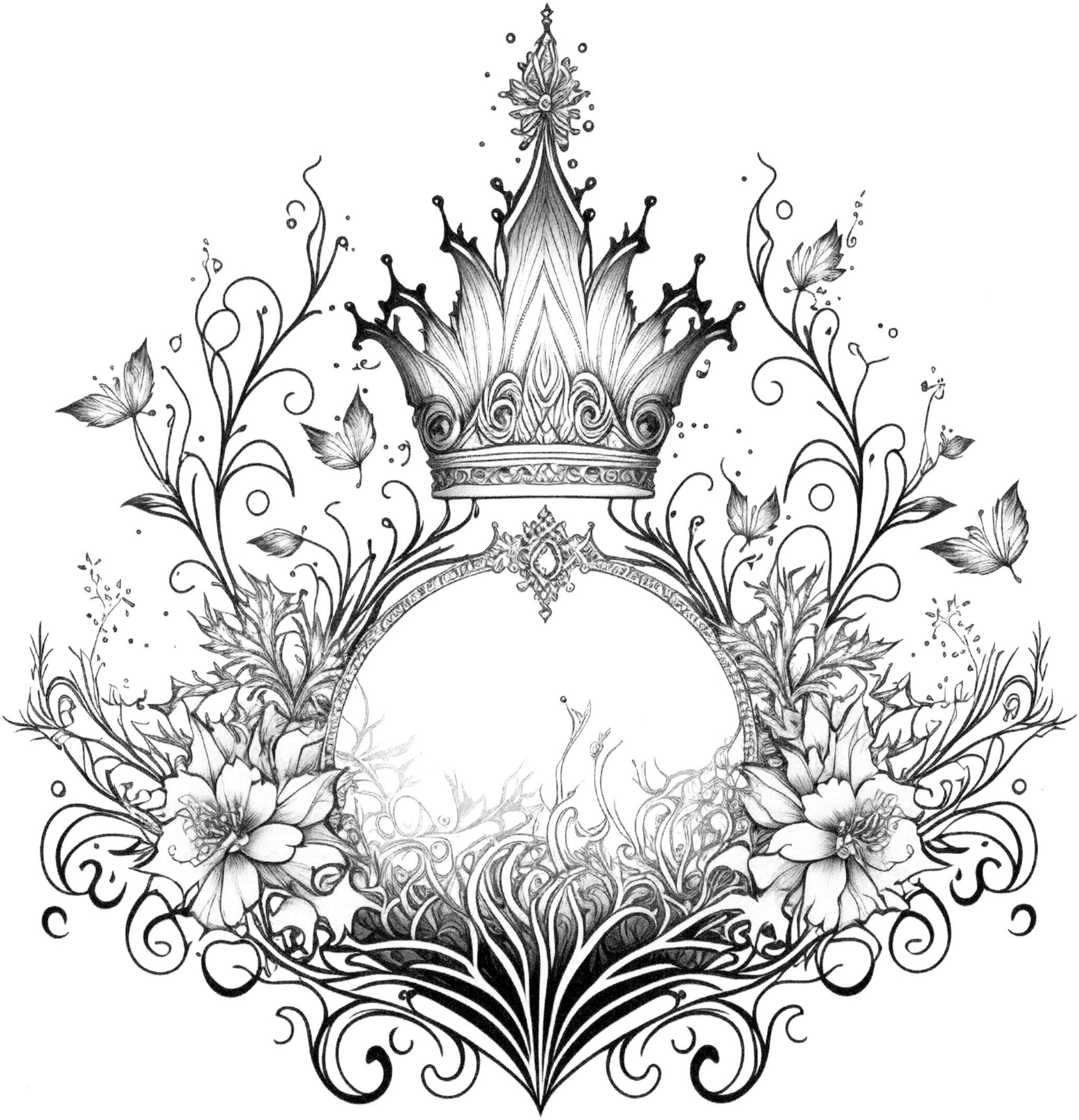

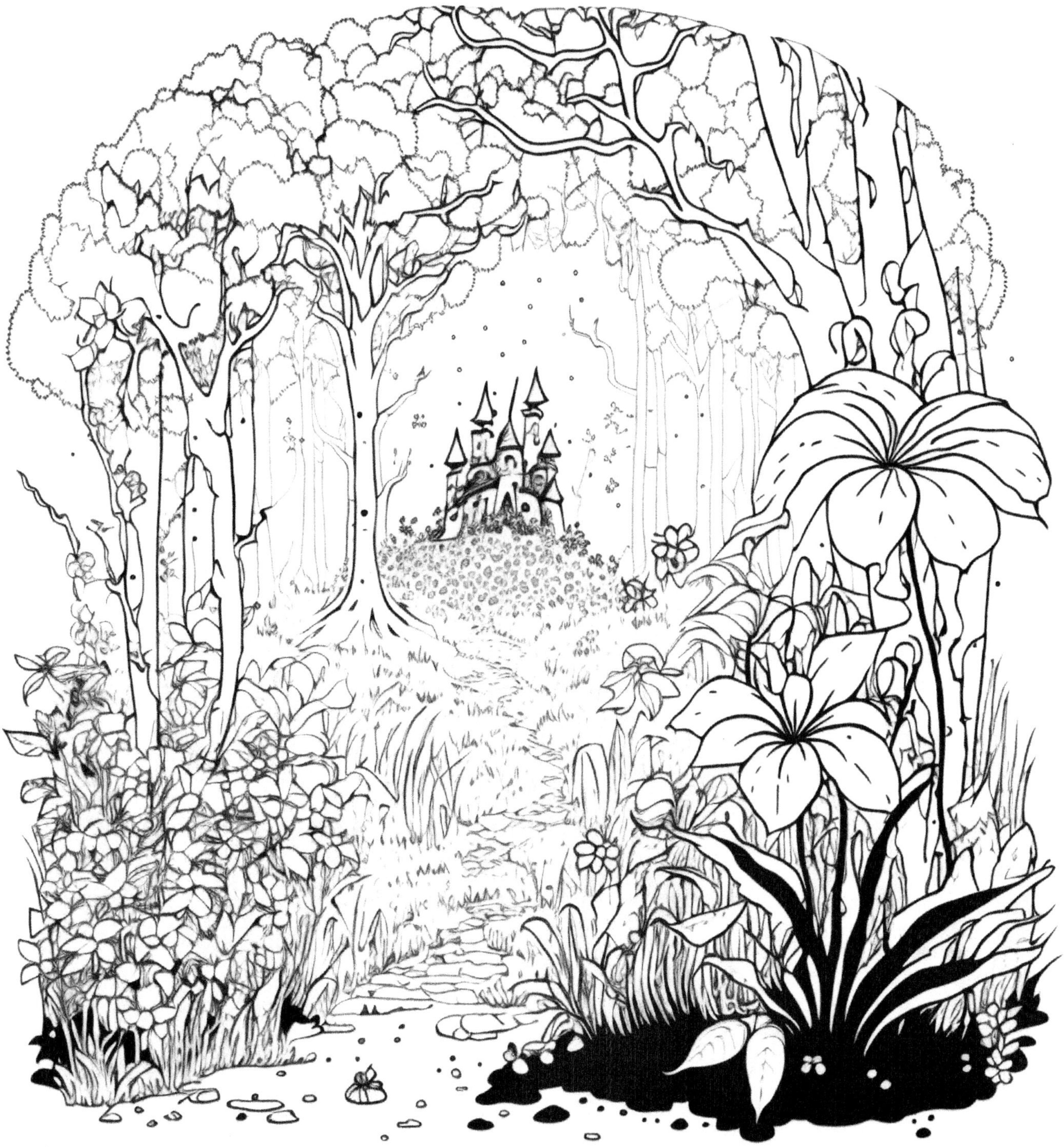

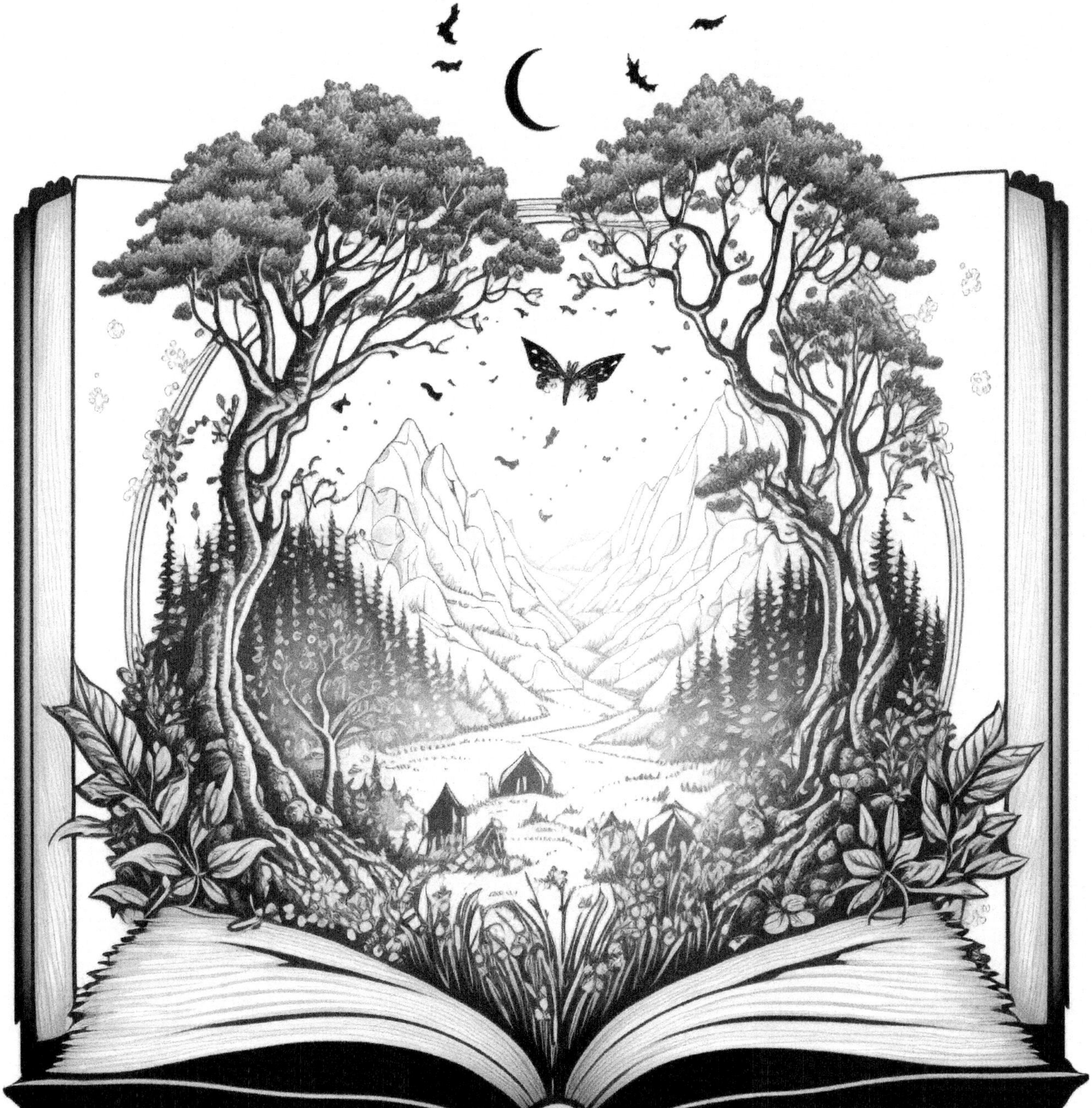

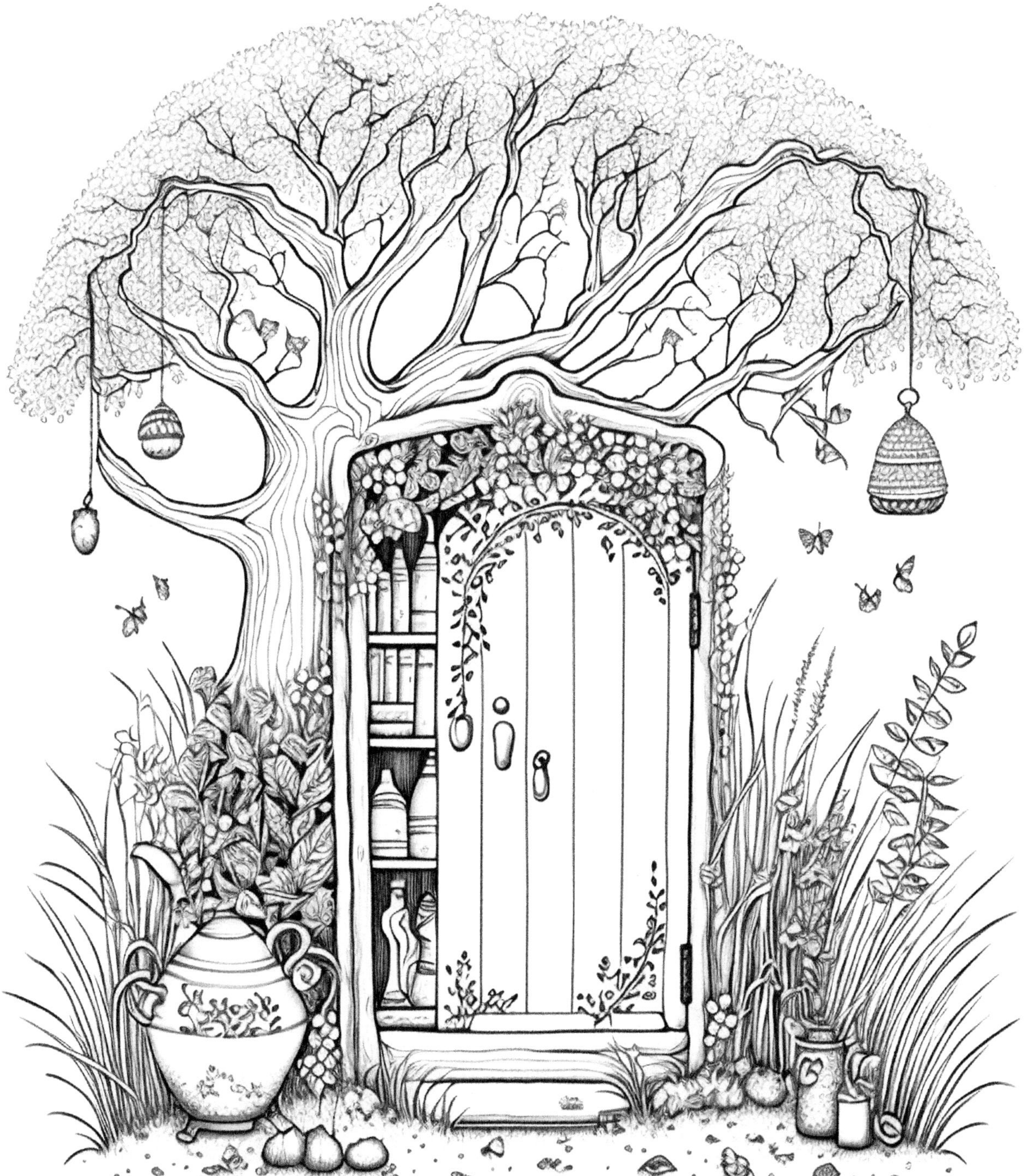

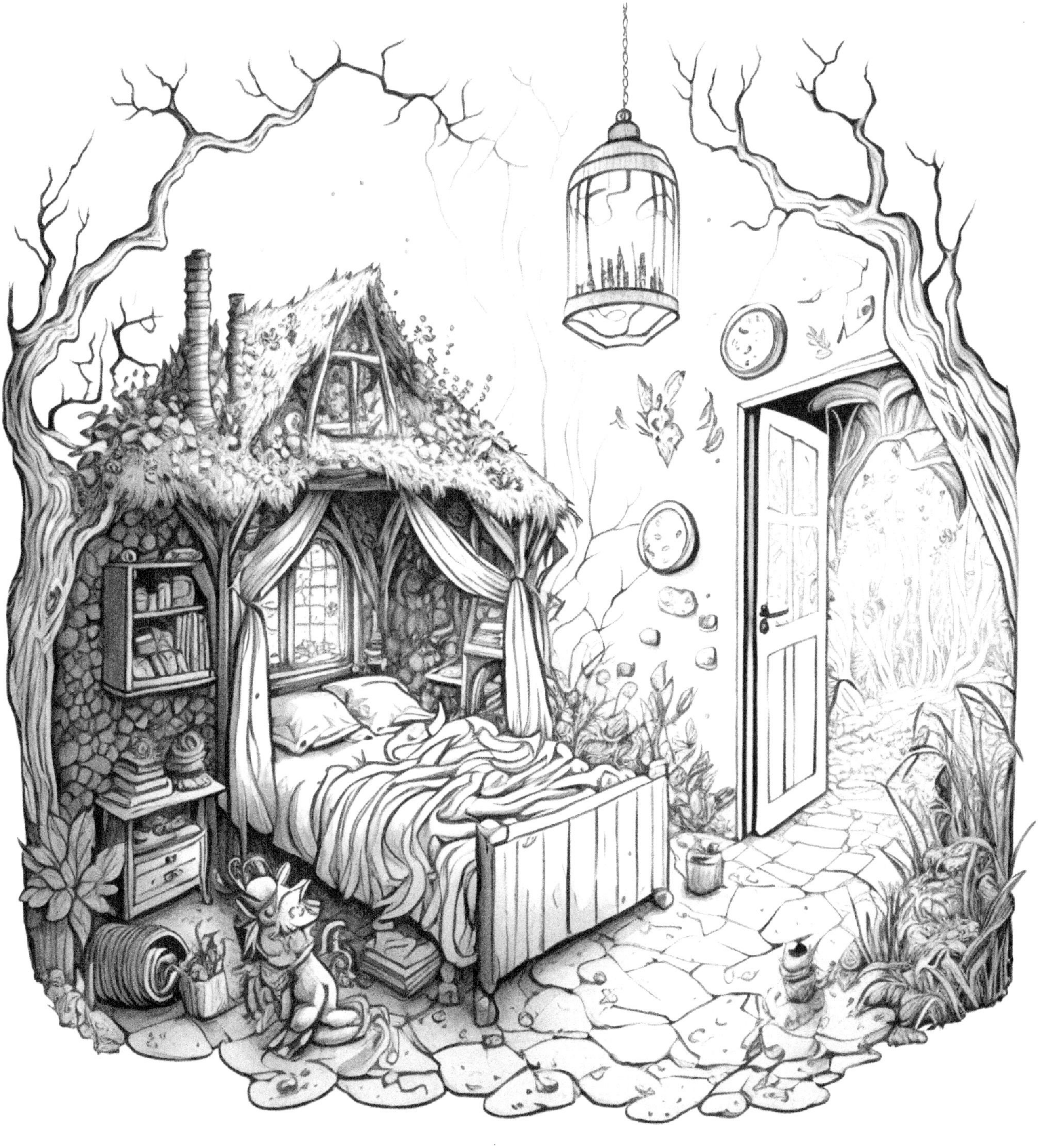

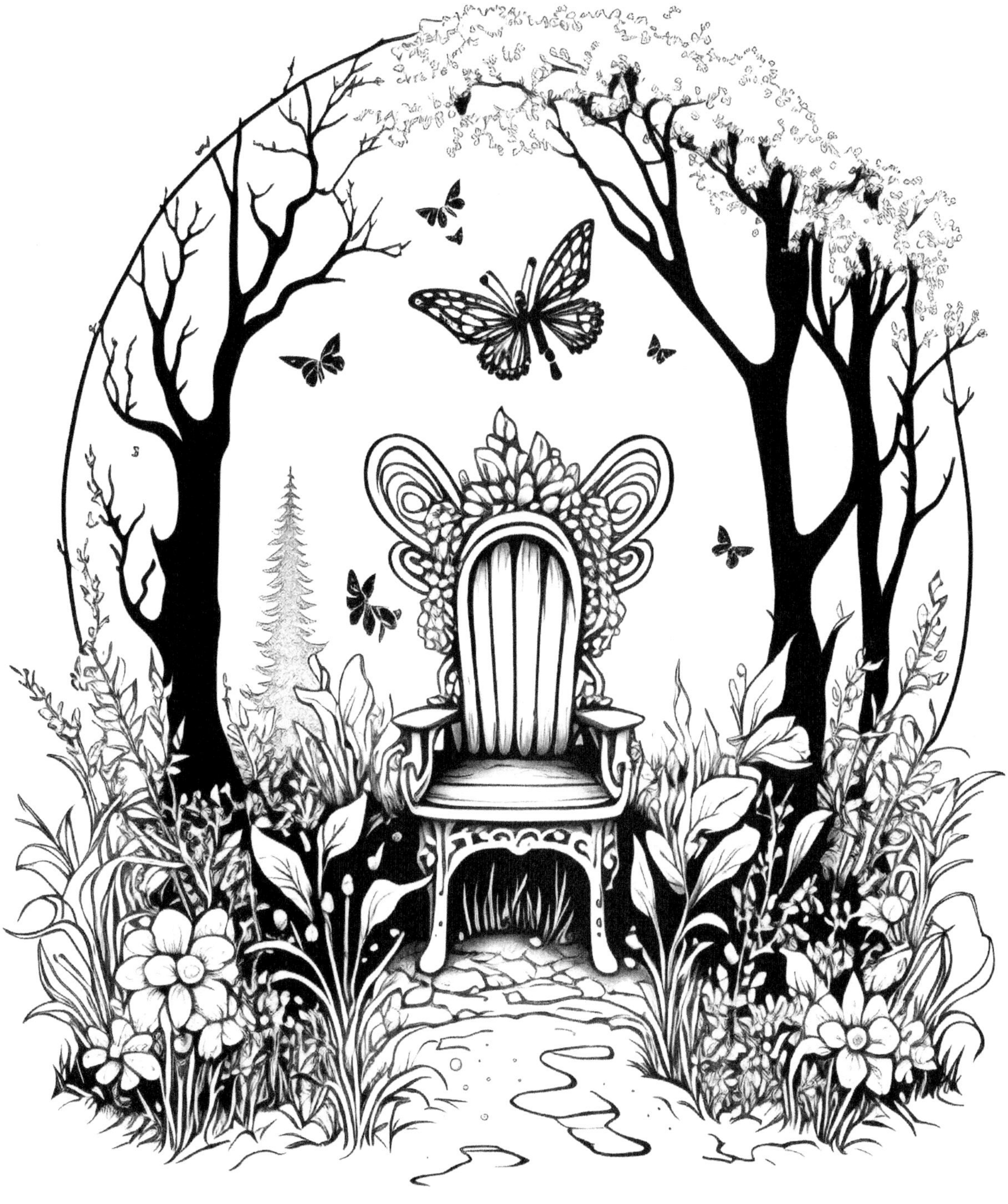

COLOR TEST SHEET

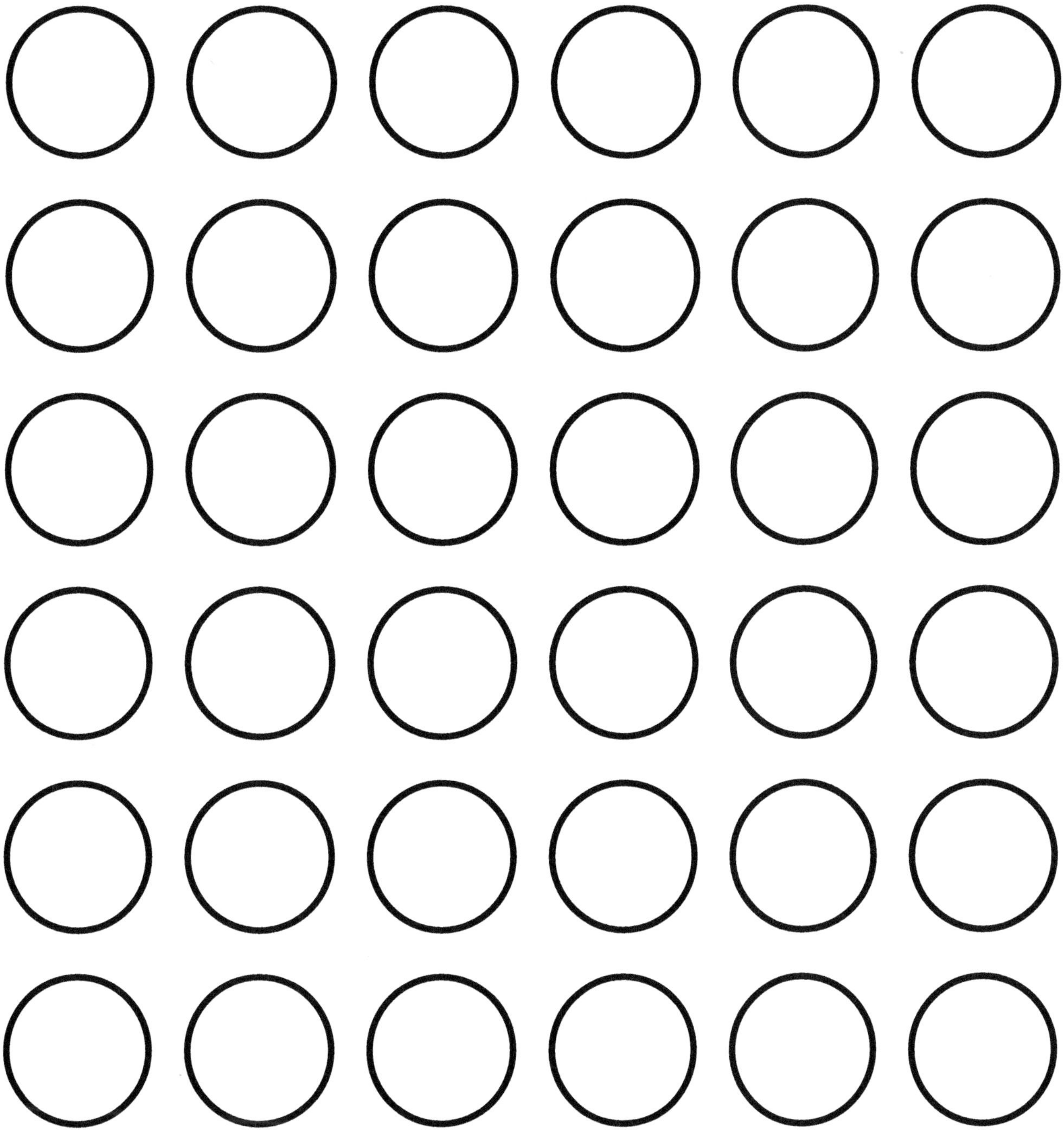

COLOR TEST SHEET

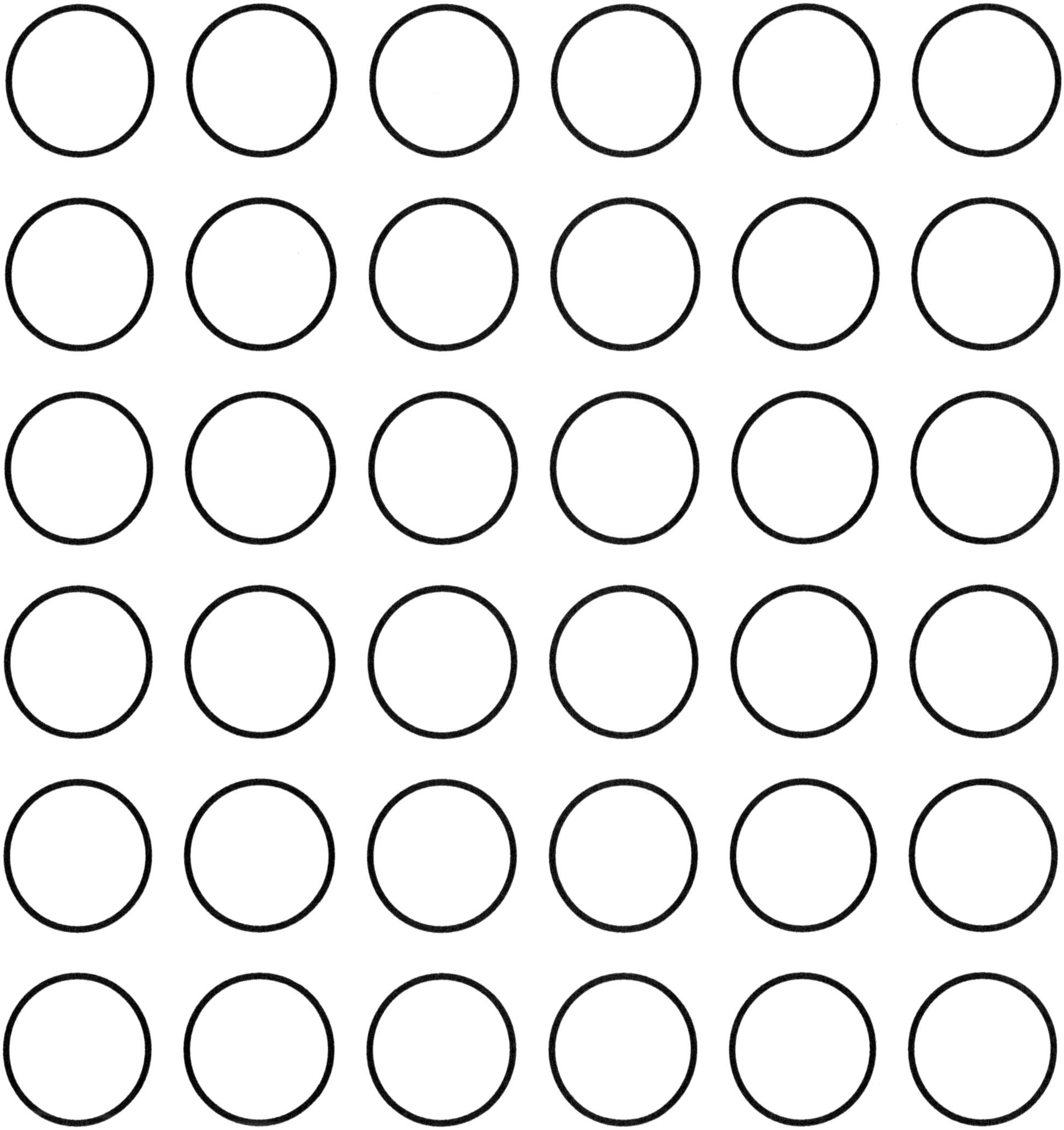

Printed in Great Britain
by Amazon

18718434R00052